Lessons from my Dog

Faith-Lifters that Bless and Build Believers

by

Nick Watson

Nick Watson Prophetic Power Ministries

youcanprophesy@gmail.com

www.youcanprophesy.com

Lessons from my Dog

Critical Ideas that Raise and Build Believers

Nick Watson

Nick Watson Prophetic Power Ministries
yourcanprophesy@gmail.com
www.youcanprophesy.com

Lessons from my Dog

ISBN 978-0-9943012-1-5

Copyright © by Nick Watson.

All rights reserved. No part of this book may be reproduced or transmitted in any form or by any means, electronic or mechanical, including photocopying and recording or by any information storage and retrieval system, without permission from the author.

Published by Nick Watson Prophetic Power Ministries.

Brisbane. Australia. 4178.

ENDORSEMENTS

Australia

Pastor Nick Watson broke new ground with his recent book, "You Can Prophesy – Supernatural. Simple. Safe." The book was straight forward, practical and releasing. His latest book is just as impacting and provides insight and wisdom which if applied will bring release to every person who reads it. As I read the book I was encouraged, inspired and motivated to apply the principles it espouses. I highly recommend you read the book and learn from Pastor Nick's personal understanding of profound scriptural principles.

Wayne Swift

National Leader, Apostolic Church Australia; Senior Pastor, Church 1330. Scoresby. Victoria. Australia.

Firstly I loved it! – great revelation and content with strong Scriptural foundation and support evidenced right throughout the text. The chapters cover a good diversity of subjects with good use of simple illustrations. I like the application questions and Faith Declarations at the end of each chapter. For me as a preacher, it is certainly a great resource for messages, or preaching thoughts.

Gary Swenson

State Ministries Director,
Australian Christian Churches (previously Assemblies of God)
Queensland and Northern Territory

With sound biblical teaching and a welcome blend of practical application and insight, Nick Watson writes on subjects in which he is well and truly qualified. Nick thinks deeply yet writes simply and his written communication is warm and encouraging, as he is in person. I commend this book to you as a worthy addition to our body of knowledge on the essential subject of Christ-honouring contemporary ministry.

Tim Jack

National Ministries Director, Apostolic Church Australia
Senior Pastor, Christies Beach, Adelaide.

As a minister of the Gospel for over 35 years I have learned to value good, sound teaching. So it is with pleasure that I recommend Nick Watson's new book. Nick is a seasoned prophet and pastor that understands the battles and trials we face daily and I believe his book will prove a blessing in practical teaching on overcoming these adversities of life.

Dr. Col Stringer

Author of 20 Christian books,
President International Convention of Faith Ministers, Australia.

This book is a Biblical gold mine; written to inform truthfully and experientially its readers with life-changing Biblical principles for an exciting, fruitful, loving obedient, Christ-filled "Life!" Throughout the reading of this easy, comfortable, yet exciting writing style of Nick's, he keeps me turning the pages until I become time and again overcome by the wealth of confirmation and witness in my spirit of the treasure truths that are so beneficially needed in our lives at all times.

Rosemary Renninson

International Devotional Writer/Speaker. Moe. Vic. Australia

Nick has written a book for the intellect, the emotions and the spirit of every person.

He captures your attention with truths that are applicable to every area of your life, leaving you wanting to continue reading. His personal and biographical anecdotes give the book authenticity and humility. The practical aspects of the book, from scripture application, faith declaration and study questions in each chapter allow for personal reflection and growth.

Thanks Nick.

Ted Evans

Pastor, Influencers Church, North Campus, Adelaide. South Australia.
International itinerant Singer, Song Writer, Worship Leader and Speaker.

I would recommend this book to anyone wishing to evaluate their progress in the Christian life, but especially for those who desire a deeper understanding of what it means to be a Christian. This book covers a range of foundational principles and practices for anyone wishing to learn about and live the Christian life. It is Bible based, with a natural flow that makes it easy to read and understand. The author has used many real life examples, which are both challenging and inspirational. I really enjoyed the read.

Kerrie Price

Author of Answer the Call: The How-to Book for Christians
and Pastor (ret.) The Rock Christian Church,
Capalaba. Queensland. Australia.

As I read through this book, I found myself presented with one of the best put together believers manuals for facing adversity, overcoming them and living a victorious Christian life. In the Word of God, believers are encouraged to fight the good fight of faith. This book goes to show you how you can fight, overcome and walk in victory over offence and various challenges in different parts of our lives. The message in the book is presented in an easy to understand set of tools and biblical guidelines well balanced from Scriptures. I would highly recommend it to leaders as teaching tools and all believers as a life manual on living a victorious Christian life.

Jimmy Njino

Senior Pastor, Victory Life Church, Toowoomba, Queensland. Australia

Nick Watson's natural ability to illustrate Biblical truth brings the principles, purposes and promises of God to life. In the 30 years I've known Nick, I've been challenged and inspired many times by his discerning approach to scripture and ministry with a prophetic edge. Between the covers of his latest book, readers will find refreshing for the soul and signposts towards an enriched life in Christ.

Neil Johnson

20Twenty Radio Host, Vision Radio Network, Queensland. Australia

USA

This is a book I enjoyed and will refer to again and again. For many years I have studied and taught pastoral ministry and done my best to be a good practitioner. This book would have been so helpful! Nick get this published and I will do my best to get it into as many hands I can.

Philip Underwood

Previously National Leader, Apostolic Churches, New Zealand; Senior Pastor (ret.) Cornerstone Church, Philadelphia. PA. USA

Nick Watson's new book lives up to its name! I found it very inspiring. You will find your faith lifted as you read each chapter. It is clear that he is not simply an author, but he has been a faithful pastor for decades. That pastoral grace comes through as Nick shepherds you into a stronger, more vibrant faith that works in every-day life. Enjoy reading Overcoming Faith Food Snack Pack as a solidly biblical and practical encouragement to strengthen your faith in Christ!

R. Sonny Misar

Author, "Journey to Authenticity".
Senior Pastor, Living Light Church. Winona. Minnesota. USA

Nick, your new book is awesome! I really enjoyed it. Nick Watson, through this book, will stir and inspire you to take hold of the God given purpose for your life. As you read, you too like myself, will be empowered to maximize your potential and possibilities. In the pages of this book, you will discover many necessary keys to unlocking what you are called to do and to be, and how to embrace who you are and most importantly whose you are. It is so refreshing to see key principles expounded on that will catapult believers into their destinies and empower them to walk it out with great freedom your book. A must read!!!

Tony Thompson

Snr. Pastor of Glory City Church, Atlanta. GA. USA
and founder of Tony Thompson Ministries International

With enthusiasm and an energetic perception Nick Watson shares how to enjoy God's wisdom and truth. Lessons from my Dog: 34 Faith-Lifters to Bless and Build Believers provides a practical resource that teaches how to pursue holiness and God's best. You will be blessed.

Laura Petherbridge

Author and Speaker, www.LauraPetherbridge.com,
www.TheSmartStepmom.com

Nick's experience as a gifted pastor and prophetic voice gives clear understanding in this easy to read guide of activating faith in the life of every believer. By walking through God's promises in Scripture Nick reveals wisdom and keys to activating a supernatural life. He allows everyone to be equipped in understanding their true identity and authority as a believer and then become empowered by the Holy Spirit to see the miraculous in their life today. You too can move from a simple intellectual faith to begin tapping into an abundance of miracle-working authority by unleashing the power of God's glory in the earth.

Rev. David Ramer M.Div

Snr Ps. Glory Fire Church, Lake Mary, FL. USA.

New Zealand

Nick's book is full of great material and reads well. I'd describe it as a wonderful discipleship tool. I enjoy working through this sort of material with my staff team – it grows big people. Well done!!

Sheridyn Rogers

Senior Pastor, Network Leader, Activate churches, NZ

Canada

Nick, I believe the subject matter in your books is very timely considering the percentage of people suffering from the consequences of leading stress filled lives. I am reminded of the scripture, "He sent His word and healed them, and delivered them from their destructions."(Psalm 107:20). I like your use of scripture to provide the antidote to the toxic outcomes of anxiety, and the fear based passivity that we are apt to indulge when facing real life crises. It is a very helpful devotional tool. I look forward to seeing it in print.

John Kirstensen

Apostle and Senior Pastor, Elim City Church, Peterborough, Ontario
and member of National Leadership Team, Apostolic Churches of Canada.

United Kingdom

Nick's book is not only easy to read but one which is practical, has depth and encourages genuine discipleship. This book contains a good mix of Holy Ghost revelation, biblical fact and principles. This book poses simple yet effective principles of discipleship that will open our lives to God's favour and His anointing.

Chris Wickland

Senior Pastor, Living Word Church. Fareham. England.

FOREWORD

Reading through this book, my heart rejoiced in the wisdom that came through the pages. This is a book of wisdom – and a gift to all believers, but particularly for those called to ministry. And I believe the Holy Spirit has inspired Nick to write this as an inheritance for the next generation of believers.

With many wonderful quotes and anecdotes, Nick imparts to us the blessing of many lessons learned through his years of ministry experience. There are many keys to be discovered by the reader about how to walk in wisdom. Prompting us with revelations and thought provoking stories, Nick has given us a gift that releases hope and help that, if applied, will cause you to walk in greater wisdom and favour.

One chapter had me "Amen-ing" aloud. Take time to absorb and apply the wonderful truths Nick has to share and you will be better for it!

Katherine Ruonala

Author of "Living in the Miraculous: How God's Love is Expressed Through the Supernatural"

Senior Leader of Glory City Church Brisbane and Apostolic oversight of the the International Glory City Church Network. Founder and Faciliator of the Australian Prophetic Council.

www.katherineruonala.com

DEDICATION

My four dedications of this book are:

- To the Lord Who has partnered with me in many ways to write it.

- To my wife Lynne and our family of four generations.

- To the people who have encouraged me in ministry, so that I can pay-it-forward.

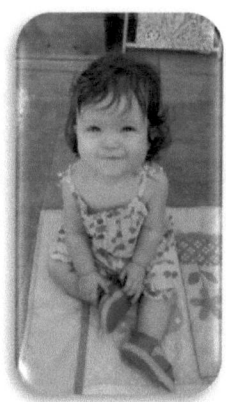

- To my great-granddaughter Riley who has inspired all us previous generations by her peace, joy, beauty and hunger for learning and growth.

ACKNOWLEDGEMENTS

I thank my amazing wife and the love of my life, Lynne, for being my indispensable partner in life and in ministry.

My thanks also go to all those who have helped me put this book together. Firstly, my chief editor John MacFarlane without whose skills and efforts this book would not have come into reality.

Secondly, my proof-reading family and friends Pastor Robert Couper, Elizabeth Scrimshaw, Barbara Hodgman, Lynne Watson and Bronwyn Cunningham.

Special mention and gratitude goes to Lisa Watson of the Printing Well, Wynnum for her sensational design of my book covers and other printing help she donated towards this project. *www.theprintingwell.com.au/*

AUTHOR'S CHOICE

I have made two non-traditional choices in this book. Firstly, I have deleted the definite article "the" from the Name of Holy Spirit, because I want Him to become more personal to my readers. Secondly, I have capitalised a lot of pronouns (such as "Him"), in order to give the Lord the honour He is due and to make clear Who the pronoun represents.

BIBLE QUOTATIONS

Unless stated otherwise, all Bible quotations in this book are taken from:

The Holy Bible, New International Version®, NIV® Copyright © 1973, 1978, 1984, 2011 by Biblica, Inc.® Used by permission. All rights reserved worldwide.

Other versions quoted:

King James Version. Public Domain.

The Amplified Bible. Zondervan Bible Publishers. © 1965. 24th reprinting – April, 1982

Scripture quotations marked ESV are from *The Holy Bible, English Standard Version*® (ESV®), copyright © 2001 by Crossway, a publishing ministry of Good News Publishers. Used by permission. All rights reserved.

Scriptures marked ISV are taken from the *Holy Bible: International Standard Version*®. Copyright © 1996-forever by The ISV Foundation. ALL RIGHTS RESERVED INTERNATIONALLY. Used by permission.

The Jerusalem Bible. DARTON, LONGMAN and TODD Ltd. And Doubleday and Company. London. 1968.

The Holy Bible, New Living Translation, copyright ©1996, 2004, 2007 by Tyndale House Foundation. Used by permission of Tyndale House Publishers, Inc., Carol Stream, Illinois 60188. All rights reserved.

The Living Bible copyright © 1971 by Tyndale House Foundation. Used by permission of Tyndale House Publishers Inc., Carol Stream, Illinois 60188. All rights reserved.

New American Standard Bible®, Copyright © 1960, 1962, 1963, 1968, 1971, 1972, 1973, 1975, 1977, 1995 by The Lockman Foundation Used by permission."

(www.Lockman.org)

New King James Version®. Copyright © 1982 by Thomas Nelson, Inc. Used by permission. All rights reserved."

Weymouth New Testament in Modern Speech. Third Edition 1913. (Public Domain)

Contents

Benaiah: Overcoming Adversity 22
Why Make Faith Confessions? 27
Sarah: God gives abilities 33
Gideon: Overcoming the Odds 39
Joshua and Jonah: Overcoming the Enemy Outside and Within 47
John the Baptist: When God does not do what we want Him to do 55
Get Godly Wisdom and Make Good Decisions 60
3 Kinds of Forgiveness 75
Faith 83
You can be Strong 90
God Who balances the scales 99
Psalm 23 107
How to have a Healthy Soul: *More like Jesus and More Joy* 115
How to have a Healthy Soul: *Train your Mind* 122
How to have a Healthy Soul: *Tame Your Tongue; Move On; Serve Others* 131
Essential Christian Qualities: *Love and Holiness* 140
Essential Christian Qualities: *Faith, Wisdom and Hope* 146
24 hour Prayer to Save a Multitude 153
Defeating the Disappointment Spiral 158
Praising our Covenant-Keeping Lord 169
The Lord's Banner Over You 176
Being Led by Holy Spirit 180
Forgiveness and Healing *in Psalm 103:1-3* 188
Freedom from Depression; Satisfaction and Renewal *in Psalm 103:1-5* 198
5 Steps to Forgiving Others 208
5 More Steps to Forgiving Others 216
What Jesus did at Easter 224

How to Treat Holy Spirit	238
Holy Spirit, our Standby: *From Atmosphere to Action*	250
Healing *and* Salvation	257
Faith Confessions *Make a Difference*	268
Journey to Double Portion: *Gilgal*	276
Journey to Double Portion: *Bethel, Jericho and Jordan*	286
Lessons from my Dog: *a Wedding Message*	297

INTRODUCTION

This book is the result of years of walking with the Lord in pastoral, teaching and prophetic ministry. It is a topical collection of life-transforming and equipping messages that cover a variety of subjects.

These are Holy Spirit inspired revelations, Biblical teachings, testimonies and illustrations that have proven fruitful in the lives of many people during my years as Senior Pastor of a thriving Spirit-filled, Apostolic church and travelling prophetic minister.

They will help you develop your God-given potential in Christ and equip you to fulfil your ministry that the Lord has assigned to you, by doing the good works of love and faith that He prepared in advance for you to do. (Ephesians 2:10).

I am honoured by the affirming comments of my anointed, experienced and internationally significant endorsers. Their reviews have confirmed to me that this book, and the four smaller books which have been generated from it, are going to meet needs, change lives, multiply ministry, equip believers, build their faith and fulfil the purposes that the Lord entrusted to me when He anointed me as an author.

My prayer is that as you read and complete the end section of each chapter, you will receive an impartation and increase of anointed giftings and abilities as Elisha did when he was hungry for a double portion of Elijah's ministry.

1 Benaiah: *Overcoming Adversity*

³⁵ So do not throw away your confidence; it will be richly rewarded. ³⁶ You need to persevere so that when you have done the will of God, you will receive what He has promised.

Hebrews 10:35-36

Benaiah was one of David's best warriors. A local village was being terrorised by a marauding lion. They asked Benaiah to help kill the beast.

On the day arranged, when he woke up, Benaiah realised that it was a bitterly cold day. So, he decided to stay in bed and he never helped the villagers.

That is not true.

He thought: "Those people need me, so off I go."

As he walked toward the village, it started snowing. So, Benaiah turned around and went home to the cosy open fire in his living room.

That is not true.

He thought: "More people will die or be seriously injured if I turn back. So, onward I go."

When he got close to the village, Benaiah fell into a lion trap which the villagers had dug. They had covered the pit with leaves and branches, which were now disguised even further by a light covering of snow.

Benaiah thought: "I knew this was not the Lord's Will for me to stick my nose into other people's business. It was just my idea to come. God has been trying to tell me all the time that I shouldn't be going on this mission."

That is not true.

Benaiah would have thought. "Lord, this is Your mission. You have made me a defender of Your people. So, this is my God-given mission and I expect You to help me overcome all obstacles to make these, Your people, safe."

After some time, during which Benaiah was praying, praising, exercising, practicing his skills in warfare and digging some handholds and footholds in the wall of the pit, the lion dropped into the very same pit.

Benaiah thought: "Oh no, here we go again. My day has gone from bad to worse. Now I'm trapped in a pit with this big, hungry beast, who is going to have me for lunch. I wish I had stayed home. I really must be out of the Will of God, even though all this time I thought I was doing His Will."

Of course he didn't think like that.

Rather, Benaiah thought: "Praise God, You have answered my prayers and I give You glory because You care for Your people so much that You have delivered this lion into my hands." Then he would have said to the lion, something like David said to Goliath in 1 Samuel 17:45-47: "Lion, you are going down right now, in the Name of the Lord."

That is why the Bible says in 1 Chronicles 11:22 that Benaiah "went down into a pit on a snowy day and killed a lion."

What about you?

What does it take for you to have a bad day?

What does it take to divert you from your life's purpose?

How much do you trust the Lord's covenant partnership with you when times get tough?

Do you believe that God plus one, namely you, is a majority?

Do you believe that through faith in God, you can overcome not just one adverse thing, but a whole series of adverse events?

Lessons From My Dog

If God be for you, who or what can be successful against you?

One of the great lessons the Lord has taught me is this: persistence overcomes enemy resistance. In fact, persistence overcomes all resistance.

Persistence overcomes all resistance

The corollary to this is that God is faithful to us in all seasons and situations.

If one thing goes wrong (it's bitterly cold), don't think God has left you or you are out of His Will.

If another thing goes wrong (it starts snowing), don't think God has left you or you are out of His Will.

If something else goes wrong (you fall into a pit), don't think God has left you or you are out of His Will.

If even a fourth or fifth or sixth thing goes wrong (such as a hungry lion dropping in for lunch unannounced), don't think God has left you or you are out of His Will.

God is always faithful.

However, you have to make sure that you are living in His Will, which means according to His Word; and make sure you learn how to hear the Voice of God on a personal and lifestyle basis, so that you are indeed being led by His Spirit.

The wonderful thing about the day of grace in which we live is that God is faithful, even when we are not (2 Timothy 2:13); but, don't become presumptuous about that. Don't put God to the test. (Matthew 4:7).

Of course, my story is not told in the Bible. There is just a one-sentence summary of what happened. So, I want to expand the illustration by imagining that Benaiah had four friends who agreed to come with him on this dangerous mission.

One of them, Levi, didn't turn up on the morning because it was too cold. Another, Nahshon, got cold feet just as they were about to leave but covered up his feelings of fear and inconvenience by saying he would stay home and safeguard the people of Benaiah's village.

A third, Jesher, gave up the cause when it started snowing. He said he was concerned that it might crush his tent and he had better get home to protect his family.

How do you react when your supporters turn back? Does it influence you to quit? Are you like Jesus Who set His face like a flint to fulfil His Father's purpose, no matter how many scattered, no matter who betrayed him?

Benaiah's fourth friend lasted all the way until he heard the lion's roar and Benaiah fell into the pit. Hezron said: "I'll go for help"; but Benaiah did not see him again that day. He went the long way back to Benaiah's village, rather than the short way to reach the endangered villagers, because he was afraid to go any closer to that hungry, roaring lion.

Let me ask you: Is your faith strong enough to stand the test of people letting you down? Are you like the old song: "I have decided to follow Jesus, no turning back, no turning back. Though none go with me, yet still I'll follow, no turning back, no turning back?"

What is one thing you have learned from this teaching?

What is one thing you can do to implement this teaching?

Faith Declaration:

I thank You Lord for Your covenant partnership in my life. I declare that in Christ I can, and by faith I will, do all the things I need to do in order to live a satisfying, successful and un-selfish life. I praise You, Lord because I can be strong in You, even when I feel weak or people around me are weak, because Christ in me strengthens me. I declare in Jesus' Name that Your faithfulness will sustain me and Your Spirit empower me to stay the course, to fulfil my mission and to win the victory, because my battles are Your battles and victory belongs to the Lord. Amen

.

2 Why Make Faith Confessions?

It is written: "I believed; therefore I have spoken." Since we have that same spirit of faith, we also believe and therefore speak
2 Corinthians 4:13

We all know, from both good and bad experiences, that words can heal, help or hurt. The important thing to understand is that your words can not only heal, help or hurt your listeners, but yourself as well, because you also hear what you say. We cannot control what other people say, but every Christian must learn how to take control of his own mind, moods and mouth.

"The tongue has the power of life and death,..."
Proverbs 18:21a

[12] Whoever of you loves life and desires to see many good days, [13] keep your tongue from evil and your lips from speaking lies.
Psalm 34:12-13

The Hebrew word for "evil" used by the Psalmist has these various meanings; through them, the Lord is telling us what kinds of words to not speak: bad, disagreeable, malignant; unpleasant, causing pain, unhappiness, misery; evil, displeasing; of low value; sad, unhappy; unkind, vicious in disposition or temper; ethically bad, wicked. So, if you want to love your life and see many good days, learn to not use words that fit into any of those negative categories.

Your words have power and they can do both harm and good. God wants you to use them for good, but the devil wants you to use them for harm. Believers who build enjoyable relationships and enduring ministries harness the positive power of their tongue.

What we speak is a matter of choice. God wants us to choose to speak for His glory and for the blessing and benefit of people. He wants us to reject being the mouthpiece of the devil or this world.

> *[10] And so blessing and cursing come pouring out of the same mouth. Surely, my brothers and sisters, this is not right! [11] Does a spring of water bubble out with both fresh water and bitter water?*
>
> *James 3:10-11*

Our words must be like living water perfumed with grace, not bitter water laced with acid.

One thing you can be sure of is that you will reap the consequences of how you choose to use your tongue.

> *From the fruit of his lips a man is filled with good things as surely as the work of his hands rewards him.*
>
> *Proverbs 12:14*

Just as your hands or work ethic can lead you to prosperity or poverty, so will the words of your mouth affect the quality of your life.

If you are a person who speaks positively, people will be attracted to you. Having a fault-finding, blame-shifting and critical tongue will ruin the quality of your life and relationships. It will also sabotage not only your own potential and destiny, but also that of any other people who are damaged by your negative words.

Why Make Faith Confessions?

I have included this chapter (a) to remind you of how powerful your words are; and (b) to explain why the faith confessions I have included in every chapter are an important way for you to gain positive outcomes by activating the principles God has given me to share with you in this book.

I challenge you:

(i) to go on a thirty-day verbal fast from negativity;

(ii) to speak only that which encourages and blesses yourself and others during that time; and,

(iii) to say out loud, in a personalised way, the promises of God on a regular basis, for the rest of your life. You personalise the Scriptures, for example, by changing the "he" to "me" or inserting your name into the verse.

If you want to grow in faith and see the blessings and miracles you are believing for, you simply must come into agreement with what God's Word says to you and about you.

If you do not agree with God and His Word, then you will not receive what He has freely and already (past tense) given you in Christ. You can literally talk yourself out of your blessing. You can talk yourself out of your miracle; or, you can choose to talk yourself into your blessing, you can choose to talk yourself into your miracle, as the Bible teaches you to do. It's your choice and you will reap the result of that choice, positively or negatively.

The words we say are an expression of our faith. Speaking is one of the ways by which we put our faith in action. When we speak out what God's Word says about our mind, body, finances, relationships, circumstances, ministry and future it brings us into partnership with God, because we are in alignment with His Will for us. (1 John 5:14–15).

We all know that creation did not happen until God spoke it into being (as in Genesis chapter 1). It is important to realise that Holy Spirit was hovering over the earth, but nothing happened until God spoke.

Lessons From My Dog

This is also true for many Christians. Holy Spirit is hovering over their lives but nothing miraculous is happening because they are not speaking God's Word over their own lives. Speaking God's Word over your life is what turns Holy Spirit atmosphere into Holy Spirit action.

This principle is taught in both the Old and New Testaments. God Himself initiated it.

> [22] *The LORD said to Moses,* [23] *"Tell Aaron and his sons, 'This is how you are to bless the Israelites. Say to them:*
>
> [24] *"The LORD bless you and keep you;* [25] *the LORD make his face shine on you and be gracious to you;* [26] *the LORD turn his face toward you and give you peace."* [27] *"So they will put My Name on the Israelites, and I will bless them.*
>
> *Numbers 6:22-27*

Notice the word "how" in verse 23. The Lord was teaching them a method by which, if they implemented it, they would be blessed. The method involved a two-part process.

First, the priest had to speak the words of blessing over the people. The effect of this was to spiritually brand the people of God. This is the meaning of "put My Name on" them in verse 27. The second part was that the Lord would see all the people who had been spiritually branded by the words that were spoken over them and then He would bless them (verse 27) in accordance with what had been spoken.

Numbers 6:22-27 says, in effect: you, the Lord's New Testament priest (1 Peter 2:5 and 9), say it and God will do it.

When you speak the Word of God over your life, you spiritually brand yourself. The Lord sees what is branded on you by His Word and He will do it.

This concept of being spiritually branded for blessing is referred to by Paul in Ephesians 1:13-14. He tells his readers that after they first believe, they are secondly "marked in Him" (NIV) with Holy Spirit as their Divine Guarantee, by Whom and through faith, they will receive their inheritance, which is both in this life and throughout eternity.

The key thing to remember is that if the words are not spoken by faith and received by faith, the spiritual brand does not stick and the blessing won't be received.

What is one thing you have learned from this teaching?

What is one thing you can do to implement this teaching?

Faith Declarations:

- The Lord is my Shepherd I shall not want (Psalm 23:1)
- I can do all things through Christ Who strengthens me (Philippians 4:13)
- Through Jesus, I am adopted into the Father's Royal Family as a fully and personally loved son/daughter of God, who is worthy to receive all of God's blessings (Galatians 4:5-7)
- Through Jesus, I am made the righteousness of God in Christ. (2 Corinthians 5:21). The prayers of a righteous person are powerful and effective. (James 5:16). My prayers are powerful and effective.

3 Sarah: God gives abilities

¹¹ By faith Sarah, even though she was old and barren, received the strength to conceive, because she was convinced that the One Who had made the promise was faithful.
Hebrews 11.11 ISV

⁴ Such confidence we have through Christ before God. ⁵ Not that we are competent in ourselves to claim anything for ourselves, but our competence comes from God. ⁶ He has made us competent as ministers of a new covenant
2 Corinthians 3:4-6

The Sydney celebration of the new millennium included a dazzling fireworks display centred on the iconic Sydney Harbour Bridge. During the celebration, the word "Eternity" was displayed on the bridge. This was because of a well-known piece of Sydney history.

For 24 years the identity of the person who wrote the word "Eternity" in a beautiful copperplate script on the pavements of Sydney streets was a matter of public interest. Then one Sunday a Baptist minister caught a man in his congregation, Arthur Stace, in the act of writing his one word Gospel on a Sydney street. The mystery was solved. The identity of the sidewalk preacher was revealed. The curiosity of the public and the media was satisfied.

Lessons From My Dog

The amazing thing was that Stace was uneducated. He couldn't read. For much of his life, Arthur was a drunken, petty criminal, who spent years in jail spread over several occasions.

He got saved and heard a preacher, John Ridley MC, say: "I wish I could sound or shout (the word "eternity") to everyone in the streets of Sydney." Immediately Stace felt a powerful calling from God to be the person who would make the word "eternity", and the God of eternity, famous in Sydney.

According to a brochure prepared by J. R. Ecob for The Herald of Hope Inc. in January 2000, Stace left church that morning and bent down to begin his decades long ministry of around 33 years, in which he wrote "eternity" more than 500,000 times.

Stace said: "The funny thing is that, before I wrote it, I could hardly spell my own name. I had no schooling and I couldn't have spelled "eternity" for a hundred quid *(Note: a "quid" was an Australian pound. Today's equivalent would be around $8,000)*. But it came out smoothly, in a beautiful copperplate script. I couldn't understand it, and I still can't."

Arthur Stace is a fine example of God giving an ability to someone that they did not have. He demonstrates that the Lord empowers His people to do His work and will.

We love reading the miracles of Jesus where people received abilities they either never had or had lost; miracles, such as the blind having their sight restored, or the lame walking.

Ihor Lakatosh is a young Ukrainian boy who was so badly burned that one arm was fused to his body and he could not walk. His mother could not take care of him and so she decided to abandon him. His injuries were untreated for years, until he was accepted as a sponsored patient at Shriners Hospital for Children in Boston. On 19 June, 2014, the Huffington Post reported his interpreter quoting Ihor as saying: "Thank you I can walk. Thank you I can walk. Thank you Lord, I can walk." They noted that after so much sorrow in his life, Ihor now has a wonderful smile and often makes the sign of the cross as he is telling people his story of a life restored.

Sarah: God Gives Abilities

That is what Sarah, wife of Abraham, experienced. I believe her testimony is told in Hebrews 11:11, as written in the above ISV version. Some other versions give the credit here to Abraham, but his story is told in other places in Scripture.

Holy Spirit revealed to me that it was her story with this statement: "God gave her the ability to do something she couldn't do."

It is possible that Sarah did have the ability to bear children in her youth. If so, the Lord restored it.

God is ready, willing and able to do the same for you, in any and every area of your life, where you need a restored or new ability.

God is ready, willing and able to give you an ability you do not have, or an ability you have lost, in any and every area of life. You need to believe Him and His Word as Sarah did.

Sarah was not able to bear children. God renewed her youth, as well as Abraham's. Then she was able to carry and birth their child of promise, Isaac.

She came to the same place of fully-persuaded faith that Abraham did. (Romans 4:21). She became convinced that God meant what He said and said what He meant.

When the devil tempted Adam and Eve in the Garden, he attacked God's Word and then God's character. They fell for these two deceptions and paid a great price for their disobedience, a price all humanity has also been paying ever since.

Like Sarah, we have to come to the place of trusting God's Word and God's character, no matter how long we have been waiting for our miracle, no matter how unlikely it is to happen.

When we have this kind of fully-persuaded, convinced faith in both God's character and Word, He will give us abilities we didn't have, so we can do what we couldn't do before. Miracles will be normal for us, as they were for the apostle Peter. In Acts 3:12, after the amazing miracle of the healing of a man crippled from birth, Peter says to the assembled crowd: "Why does this surprise you?"

For centuries God has made apostles, prophets, evangelists, pastors and teachers out of farmers, housewives, fishermen, tax collectors, prisoners and whomever else He calls. The Lord has made millionaires out of what we call in Australia today "blue-collar workers." This demonstrates the well-known saying: "God doesn't call the qualified; He qualifies the called."

Holy Spirit can make you competent in any and every area of life and ministry. Yes, you will need to grow your faith. Yes, you will have to put your faith into action. Yes, you will have to renew your mind and harness your tongue. Yes, you might have to upskill yourself in the Word, the things of the Spirit, and even natural areas of knowledge and ability. When you do whatever you need to do, as Sarah did, Holy Spirit will help you step into greater levels of natural and supernatural abilities.

Recently, I read an interesting perspective on spiritual gifts, in regard to 1 Corinthians 12:11. The traditional way of understanding this verse is that Holy Spirit gives whatever gifts He decides to people. The Bible teacher I read is the first I have found in more than 38 years of Pentecostal Christianity to say that the Greek construction of the verse allows for a different translation. It can also be translated that Holy Spirit gives spiritual gifts just as the receiver determines. This is certainly in harmony with the two verses (1 Corinthians 12:31a and 14:1) that tell us we must earnestly desire spiritual gifts, especially that we might prophesy. Why would we be told to earnestly desire specific gifts, if Holy Spirit was intending to give us different ones? Selah!

When you look at the life of King David, you will see the progressive impartation of Divine abilities through the three anointings in his life.

The first, imparted by the prophet Samuel, to signal his future ministry of kingship enabled him to be a shepherd who could kill lions, bears and giants, because Holy Spirit came upon him mightily from that day forward. The anointing produced leadership and ministry capabilities in David that were not limited to his human abilities. David was empowered to be a prophetic worshipper, whose playing attracted the Presence of

God so much that it caused demons to flee from King Saul. Previously, David had been a shepherd and a worshipper; but now the anointing brought the supernatural dimension of God's abilities into his life.

The anointing empowered him to prophesy defeat to Goliath, to kill that giant and then to lead Israel's army to victory over the Philistines. His abiding anointing was sufficient for him to lead his own small army for years. David started with four hundred men, who were in distress or in debt or discontented, at Adullam. (1 Samuel 22:2). The anointing on David's life helped him to turn them into an army of giant-killers.

David's second anointing was imparted by the tribe of Judah. (2 Samuel 2:4a). This anointing increased David's leadership ability to handle more than 500,000 men of military age. (This is according to the census in 2 Samuel 24:9). In other words, David's abilities went to another level for seven and a half years.

In 2 Samuel 5:3-4, David was anointed for the third and final time. He was anointed king over all Israel. This meant that an extra 800,000 men came under David's command. He now had 1.3 million men of military age to lead. The anointing of Holy Spirit increased his abilities to another level, again. He ruled for forty years.

David's life, leadership and ministry demonstrate that the greater the anointing, the greater the capacity of the one who has been anointed.

Lessons From My Dog

What is one thing you have learned from this teaching?

_____

What is one thing you can do to implement this teaching?

_____

Faith Declaration:

Thank You Lord that it's not by my might and it's not by my power, but it's by Your Spirit that mountains, blockages, problems and limitations will be removed from my life. I praise You that I can do all things through Christ Who strengthens me. I put my trust in You to help me walk and not faint, run and not grow weary, and rise up with wings like eagles. I thank You that from today I am receiving new and greater abilities, talents, anointings and spiritual gifts to do what I could not do before. By faith I declare that Holy Spirit is enlightening and empowering me to succeed in greater ways than ever before, in every area of my life, relationships and ministry, in Jesus' Name. Amen.

_____

4 Gideon:
Overcoming the Odds

For God did not give us a spirit of timidity ..... but [He has given us a spirit] of power and of love and of a calm and well-balanced mind and discipline and self-control.
2 Timothy 1:7 AMP

The LORD turned to him and said, "Go in the strength you have and save Israel out of Midian's hand. Am I not sending you?"
Judges 6:14

In this chapter, I will show you six steps Gideon had to undertake in order to change his own life and the destiny of his family and nation.

(i) Gideon had to change his self-perspective to agree with God.

It must have been an amazing thing for fearful Gideon to be visited by an angel. It was doubly amazing when the angel said that in God's opinion fraidy-cat Gideon was a mighty man of valour. Gideon probably checked his temperature to make sure he didn't have a fever that was causing him to hallucinate. I guess that's why the Lord arranged for fire to supernaturally rise from the rock and consume the meat and bread that Gideon had offered Him as hospitality. You'd think the appearance and message of an angel would have been proof enough that God was speaking to him.

There are two things to note from the Lord's prophetic statement that referred to Gideon as a "mighty man of valour." Firstly, God doesn't put us down or use prophecy to point out our problems and weaknesses; rather, He speaks to our potential, knowing that His Word will kick-start a process of development in our lives. Secondly, take note of the word "process" I used. Gideon had a lot of changing and growing to do, before he actually became the mighty man of valour that the Lord had spoken into being over him.

The way the Lord did this was not to just flick His Divine fingers and shoo the spirit of fear out of Gideon. God gave Gideon several opportunities to face his fears and triumph over them. That's what He expects of every Christ-follower.

(ii)   Gideon had to overcome himself and his inner negatives.

One of the ways Gideon did that was in obedience to the Lord's command to: "Go in the strength that you have." (Judges 6:14). This is one of the most important principles of faith in the entire Bible. Gideon had to stop focussing on what he didn't have and use what he did have. When he did, Gideon proved that God was with him, rewarding his faith by giving him victory, success and prosperity.

(iii)   Gideon had to pull down his father's idol.

I wrote about this in my first book "You Can Prophesy – Supernatural. Simple. Safe."

Gideon's destruction of the altar of Baal is another example of prophetic action (Judges 6:25-27). Gideon could not change things on earth and gain a great victory for his people, unless and until he first got rid of the enemy's stronghold of idolatry, deception, theft, intimidation and bondage over the people of God.

I want you to notice the prophetic significance of God commanding Gideon to use the second bull. Normally the Lord always has the first and best offering. However, the second bull was seven years old, the exact age of the enemy's domination of Israel (Judges 6:1). So the sacrificial death of the seven year old bull was a prophecy of the end of the defeat and poverty God's people had experienced during the bull's lifetime. It was prophetic of the end of the enemy's domination of them.

Gideon's destruction of the pagan altar was prophetic of the breaking of demonic power over the people, and, after that spiritual victory, his courageous leadership brought about the freedom and prosperity of the entire nation for an entire generation of forty years. (Judges 8:28).

Gideon had to obey God even though he knew people would be angry with him – seriously, even dangerously, angry with him. That's a real challenge for a lot of people. But that's what it takes to be a believer. We have to do things God's way, even if we suffer for it. Sure enough, an argument broke out after Gideon tore down the idol; but his dad, Joash, quickly quenched it.

That quick victory was itself prophetic of other victories to come, because the enemy had now been stripped of the demonic spiritual power that had been aiding and abetting his evil cause.

(iv) Gideon had to learn how to yield to Holy Spirit and desire His fullness.

Holy Spirit came upon Gideon to call the tribes to war against the massive invading army. The literal Hebrew expression used in Judges 6:34 is that Holy Spirit clothed Himself with Gideon. How awesome is that. But it's not as awesome as what we New Testament believers have, which is the indwelling Presence of Holy Spirit

In the Old Testament, Holy Spirit came upon certain people at different times for specific purposes. In the New Testament, He is with each and every believer, all the time, for every good and godly purpose. Hallelujah.

As you look at this piece of history, you can see how Gideon was emboldened to blow the war trumpet by Holy Spirit "clothing" him.

Even with Holy Spirit's empowerment, Gideon still had to function in faith.

Lessons From My Dog

When, as many would describe it today, the anointing lifted, Gideon's fear got the better of him again. I don't blame him for that, because Israel was well and truly outnumbered by a combined army that had defeated them many times before.

So, Gideon puts out his two famous fleeces and in His grace and mercy, the Lord answers from Heaven to reassure Gideon of victory.

I love this Scripture:

> *For he (God) knows how weak we are; He remembers we are only dust.*
> *Psalm 103:14*

The Lord will help each and every one of us every step of the way. He is not fazed by the weakness of our humanity. However, God requires us to put our faith on the line in active partnership with Him, as Gideon did time and again.

(v) Gideon has to learn that faith is not a one-off act, but a lifestyle of obedience and taking risks for and with God.

So, Gideon has to reduce the size of his army, not once, but twice. This is military madness. If they were clearly outnumbered before, now the odds of 300 men defeating an army as thick as a locust plague, with too many camels to count, are beyond ridiculous. (Judges 7:12).

To his credit, Gideon did as the Lord had instructed him. If he had not, he would have disappeared from the pages of the Bible and God would have empowered another who would obey Him.

Now comes the most nonsensical challenge anybody could give a man, except for trained commandos, in the military situation Gideon now faced.

> *That night the LORD said, "Get up! Go down into the Midianite camp, for I have given you victory over them!* [10] *But if you are afraid to attack, go down to the camp with your servant*

Purah. ¹¹ *Listen to what the Midianites are saying, and you will be greatly encouraged. Then you will be eager to attack." So Gideon took Purah and went down to the edge of the enemy camp.*

Judges 7:9-11 NLT

The Lord says to Gideon: "if you are afraid, go down to the (enemy) camp". Wouldn't it be better if God had said: "If you are afraid, retreat a few kilometres until the time is right to attack them"? or, "If you are afraid, I will show you the 100,000 angels I have accompanying you"?

Again, Gideon demonstrates how he got control over his negative feelings and probably eradicated them completely from his life.

He subdued them by confronting them and acting in faith by doing the very opposite of what his inner negatives were pressuring him to do. This demonstrates the familiar saying: "Faith and courage are not what we do in the absence of fear, but doing the right thing despite the fear."

Gideon controlled, subdued and eradicated his negative feelings by acting in faith

It was through the history of Gideon that the Lord first showed me this principle: Every situation of fear is also an opportunity for faith.

Every situation of fear is also an opportunity for faith

When Gideon arrived at the enemy camp, where there must have been literally thousands of tents, he crept up to the very one where he can overhear the men inside. At that very moment, one is describing a divine dream, with a meaning that frightens the enemy and encourages Gideon.

What are the odds of Gideon being in exactly the right place at exactly the right time? That's what God can do for you when you are on His side and He is on yours.

(vi) Gideon has to learn that victory comes from attacking the enemy, not avoiding conflict.

Many have said: offence is the best form of defence. The Bible teaches that advancing the Kingdom of Heaven requires "violence", which means boldness and assertive, proactive faith. (Matthew 12:11).

Gideon's final test is to start the attack, by faith, using a God-given strategy and then complete the fight, until the enemy was so destroyed that they were not successful against Israel for another forty years. Hallelujah.

Now what about you? Are you ready to progressively overcome your fears and other inner negatives? Are you ready to consistently put your faith on the line according to the Word of God and the leading of His Spirit in order to partner with God to fulfil your potential and destiny?

Every Christian must exercise active faith in their various circumstances, opportunities and challenges of life. We are not to just passively wait for God to fight our spiritual enemies and overcome our different obstacles for us.

> *Be strong, all you people of the land," declares the LORD, 'and work. For I am with you,'*
> *Haggai 2:4,5*

³ Strengthen the feeble hands, steady the knees that give way; ⁴ say to those with fearful hearts, "Be strong, do not fear
Isaiah 35:3,4a

When you do the best you can and trust God to do the rest, the Lord will surely do what you cannot do.

Lessons From My Dog

What is one thing you have learned from this teaching?

What is one thing you can do to implement this teaching?

Faith Declaration:

I thank You Lord for helping me grow by overcoming my fears and other negatives and inner hindrances. Thank You for enabling me to confront and be victorious over any giant or mountain or army that is in my way. I praise You because Your Divine Partnership empowers me to do far more than I could ever do alone. I exalt You as my Champion and Lord and thank You for enabling me to achieve victory, peace and prosperity in my life, for my family and my entire sphere of influence, in Jesus' Name. Amen.

5 Joshua and Jonah:
Overcoming the Enemy Outside and Within

"The word of the Lord came to Jonah ....But Jonah ran away from the Lord..."
Jonah 1:1 and 3

... Now then, you and all these people, get ready to cross the Jordan River into the land I am about to give to them — to the Israelites.³ I will give you every place where you set your foot, as I promised Moses.... ⁵ No one will be able to stand against you as long as you live. For I will be with you as I was with Moses. I will not fail you or abandon you.
Joshua 1:2-3 and 5

Then the Lord said to Joshua, "See I have delivered Jericho into your hands along with its king and its fighting men. ... ²⁷ So the Lord was with Joshua, and his fame spread throughout the land.
Joshua 6:2 and 27

Some years ago I felt the Lord was prompting me to preach a series based on the book of Jonah. I wasn't keen on that idea. So, I did what I tell others not to do. I started asking around our church to see if I could find someone who would agree with me and give me an excuse to not preach about Jonah.

Perhaps I didn't sell my case very well. Starting with "I think God wants me to preach the book of Jonah" was probably not going to gain me many naysayers. Sure enough, pretty much the standard answer I got was: "Well, if the Lord is telling you to do it, you'd better go ahead and preach it." At least I discovered that I had taught the people to obey God.

Around this time, we had a serious church meeting of a select number of leaders. A staff member premeditatedly and without warning to me hijacked the meeting to attack me. It felt like he walked up to me with a knife in his hand and used it as Ehud did in Judges 3:19-21. It seemed like he twisted it and threw in as much salt as he could.

Somehow, on the outside, I maintained my equilibrium and got through the rest of the meeting, which you might easily surmise did not achieve any great or godly purpose.

As I drove away from the meeting, I thought "I am going to drive far out of town and stay out of contact for three days and three nights."

About fifty metres ahead of me was a set of traffic lights. I was intending to turn toward the highway and just keep on going. But in those few metres, Holy Spirit spoke to me. God said: "Be a Joshua, not a Jonah." In other words, don't run away as Jonah did. Stay here and win this battle. Don't be robbed of your (plural, meaning our whole church) Promised Land inheritance.

So, I went home and the next night, I repaired the damage done in a second meeting with all concerned.

Then Holy Spirit said: "Now, I want you to preach a series on Joshua, not Jonah." I did that and it was one of the best teaching series I ever did.

Holy Spirit said to me: Be a Joshua, not a Jonah

Can you see how the Lord knew in advance what was going to happen that negative night? Yet, He didn't save me from it. Rather, He prepared me to learn from it, grow through it and overcome it.

That's what He did with Gideon. God didn't click His fingers to take away Gideon's fears. The Lord gave him opportunities to confront his fears and overcome them by acting courageously. Gideon did so by developing a wonderful and powerful partnership with Holy Spirit. (Judges 6:34). I did the same.

Gideon won for his nation and family a generation of peace and prosperity. I and the people who teamed with me have built a lasting outpost of God's Kingdom in our area. Indeed, the people of our local church will send out the love, truth and power of God for generations to come.

I proved in those two nights, and on many other occasions when problems needed solving and miracles just had to happen, two well-known sayings: "Leadership is lonely"; and "God plus one is a majority."

If God is for us who can be against us?
Romans 8:31

When I was in high school, I had a strange way of getting to class. Instead of getting the bus that went left, in the direction of my school, I used to get an earlier bus that went right. That bus took me to a downtown stop where the girls from Smith Street Girls School used to catch their bus. One of those young ladies had caught my eye, big-time.

One day while at the bus stop with her, three guys, who were their own small gang, approached me. They threatened me by saying if they ever saw me with that girl again they would attack me.

It was not in my best interests to argue with them, when the odds were three against one. So, I enlisted the help of my two strong, athletic friends, Nick and Ziggy. A few days later, we approached the three young men, their faces dropped and their bravado left them.

Why? Because Nick, although not tall, was a very strong, athletic-looking teenager whose chest was almost as wide as the street on which we were walking and his biceps were as large as a grown man's thighs. Ziggy was so big and strong that when he walked down the street he blocked out the sun.

My three adversaries refused my invitation to settle the matter that afternoon. They accepted my peace terms unconditionally and never bothered me again.

I had realised that if I let this gang intimidate me, then I could never enjoy the freedom of getting to know that very interesting young lady and I would no longer have the freedom of my city that I enjoyed. I would have to avoid that part of town. Therefore, I acted in both faith and wisdom in order to maintain my quality of life.

The help I got from Nick and Ziggy that day is the merest fraction of the infinite help the Lord has committed Himself to giving me and every true child of His. Hallelujah! I have often illustrated the difference between God and the devil this way: God is a herd of elephants; the devil is an ant. That's sums up the level of support we have with the Lord being always on our side and by our side.

So it's as true as every other promise of God in His Word: If God is for us who or what can be against us?

The courage I got that day as a school student from having my two friends with me gives a small indication of how Joshua must have felt after he met the Lord as Commander-in-Chief of the Armies of God, meaning both angelic and Israelite on earth. (Joshua 5:13-15).

Joshua also drew courage from what the Lord had spoken to him in Joshua 1:1-9, which included the specific promise of the Lord's accompanying "Emmanuel – God with us" Presence.

> *... for the LORD your God will be with you wherever you go.*
> *Joshua 1:9*

It is a powerful thing to have your faith built by the Word of the Lord. When that Word is added to by the manifest Presence of the Lord, faith soars to far greater heights. So, we must be people of both the Word and of the Presence, if we want to take nations for and with God.

Joshua and Jonah: Overcoming the Enemy Outside and Within

Joshua did both of these. The commandment the Lord gave him, which if obeyed would ensure his ongoing prosperity and success, was to meditate on the Word of God day and night and obey it. (Joshua 1:7-8).

In Exodus 33:11 we are told that Joshua loved the Presence of God. Even after Moses left the tent where the Glory cloud of God had manifested, Joshua would stay there.

Similarly, Christians must know the Word of God personally and not think they will grow strong in the Lord on an inconsistent diet of Sunday sermons. We also have to cultivate intimacy with the Lord on a daily, not weekly or fortnightly basis. This enables us to hear God's Voice and partner with Him. Thirdly, we must put our faith on the line in practical, active ways, in obedience to the Word and as the Lord leads.

The two words translated prosperity and success in Joshua 1:8 are interesting.

The Hebrew word for prosperity is "tsachal". It literally means to advance, prosper, rush, attack or breach. In other words, if you want to prosper, you are going to have to learn how to overcome opposition and adversity. You are going to have to "get on the front foot", as our cricketing friends say. You will have to be proactive in working for a prosperous life or business or ministry.

The second Hebrew word is "sakal", which literally means to act wisely. It is mentioned four times in regard to David's success in one chapter. (1 Samuel 18:5,14,15,30). Verse 14 says that David was so successful, more successful than anyone else, because the Lord was with him. This is the very same key to success attributed to Joseph in Genesis 39:3,21,23.

So, if you want to succeed in life, you need to ask God for His wisdom in your major decisions, and you must cultivate your personal friendship and partnership with the Lord. You cannot act like the village clown or like some crazy character on a mid-morning television soap opera and expect to be successful.

The two key principles I want you to get from this chapter are in the title.

Firstly, in order to be successful in life, you must overcome the enemy within.

To be successful, you must overcome the enemy within

Jonah really did not do this, as you can see for yourself by reading chapter 4 of his book in the Bible. So, he occupies only a small part of the Bible compared to what he could have done if he had sorted himself out on the inside.

Moses missed out on the Promised Land because he didn't get control of his anger problem. In chapter 6 of my first book "You Can Prophesy – Supernatural. Simple. Safe.", I wrote: "In Exodus 17:6, Moses struck the rock in order to produce a massive amount of water, enough to satisfy two and a half million people, enough to save them from physical death in the wilderness. This was prophetic of the fact that Jesus would be struck on Calvary, so that the world might be saved from spiritual death, in the spiritual wilderness of sin.

Moses was not allowed to enter the Promised Land because he wrote a prophetic mistake into the pages of God's book. When he struck the rock a second time, instead of speaking to it, as God had commanded him, Moses effectively wrote into the bible that Jesus would be struck twice, which He wasn't. (Numbers 20:7-12). Jesus' once-only sacrifice on Calvary was more-than-sufficient for the salvation of mankind, for their restoration to relationship and partnership with God, for the stripping of the devil of his authority as the god of this world. So, God told Moses, on the second occasion, to speak to the rock, because after Calvary, all we believers have to do is speak to the Lord and every blessing and resource we need, that has all been paid for by Jesus' sacrifice and triumph, is released to us through answered prayer."

When you read Numbers 20:10 today, centuries after it was written, you can still feel the frustration and anger in Moses' words.

Moses said to them, "Listen, you rebels, must we bring you water out of this rock?" (Numbers 20:10).

In verse 12, the Lord adds another sin to Moses' disobedience. As well as dishonouring God by saying must "we" (meaning himself and Aaron, not the Lord) bring you water, the Bible says Moses was acting in unbelief when he struck the rock. He just didn't believe that speaking to the rock would produce the same result as occurred when he struck the rock in the book of Exodus.

Secondly, as we see demonstrated in Joshua's many victories to take possession of the Promised Land, we must confront the external adversities and adversaries we are faced with in life and ministry.

To be successful requires us to confront and overcome our external adversities and adversaries

Your strategy to overcome must take into account these two factors: (a) that *"our struggle is not against flesh and blood".* (Ephesians 6:12). We do not treat people in the ordinary course of our lives as our enemies; (b) the weapons we use to overcome both people and things, that are opposing our progress in line with the Will and purposes of God, are spiritual. Our weapons of succeeding over opposition and adversity are not military, nor are they the weapons the world teaches us to use against others, such as gossip and criticism. Our weapons are things such as prayer, love, faith and Godly wisdom.

What is one thing you have learned from this teaching?

What is one thing you can do to implement this teaching?

Faith Declaration:

I thank You Lord for helping me overcome my hurts and fears. I thank you that I am a Joshua, not a Jonah. I praise You for partnering with me to build a great life, family and ministry that is changing the world around me, one step and one day at a time. I declare that I will not be intimidated by people, circumstances or threats from the devil in my mind. I praise you because You have not given me a spirit of fear, but of power, love and a sound mind and self-control. Therefore, I decree that I will do all the things I need to do, in order to live a victorious, successful and prosperous life by faith and by the empowering of Your Holy Spirit.

6 John the Baptist:
When God does not do what we want Him to do

Blessed is anyone who does not stumble on account of Me.
Luke 7:23

But wisdom is proved right by all her children.
Luke 7:35

Some years ago, I was in the middle of a stressful ministry season. I did something I have done only once in more than thirty years of ministry. I called a pastor friend. I told him, I had no motivation to preach that Sunday and asked him to step in for me. Even though it was short notice, he did a great job for the Lord and our congregation.

I took off for the weekend with some teaching videos (remember them?). As I watched them over the next forty-eight hours, I got quite a kick in the rear end from the Lord.

Holy Spirit really spoke to me through John the Baptist's experience, as described in Luke 7:18-35. I realised I was upset not only with people and circumstances, but with the Lord Himself, because He wasn't doing what I wanted Him to do for me.

When John the Baptist was imprisoned, he wanted Jesus to rescue him. Who wouldn't?

Lessons From My Dog

John's frustrated expectations led him to doubt the supernatural revelation that God Himself had given him. He began to question whether Jesus really was the Messiah, even though he had received prophetic insight that Messiah was coming and a supernatural vision of Holy Spirit descending upon Jesus like a dove, when John baptised Him.

This is the same tactic the devil used in the Garden of Eden. He incited Adam and Eve to doubt God's Word and then God's character.

We are not true believers if we begin to doubt God's Word and/or character just because the Lord is not doing what we want Him to do. The quality of God's character and the truth of His Word is not dependent upon our needs or circumstances.

Jesus' message to the disciples of John was that they could tell John the proof of His Messiah-ship was that the Gospel was being preached with signs following.

It is significant that Jesus did not say anything about John's future, nor did He promise to go to the prison to visit or free John.

The first of two standout statements Jesus made that I needed to learn from was verse 23.

I had to learn to refuse to stumble in faith over things the Lord did or didn't do; or things the Lord said or didn't say; or things the Lord did for others but not for me.

John was actually, without him knowing it at the time, at the end of his ministry and near the end of his life. I think most of us would prefer to not know when that day was coming. I encourage you to pray as I do, that the Lord, by His grace, will enable you to finish well – relationally, with God and people, internally, ministerially, circumstantially, in health and in finances ... and in how and when you die.

Most of us are not in the place of nearness to death – but I gladly admit I am one of those Christians who believe that Jesus could come at any time. Therefore we should live as those who are ready to meet Him at any time.

Assuming we have a lot more life to live with and for the Lord, you need to learn, as I did, how to pass the test of both faith and character which John had to when he received Jesus' reply from his disciples.

He had to rejoice in the blessings and miracles that others were receiving from God, while at the same time not getting an answer about or a miracle for his own situation.

We have to learn to let God be God. Romans 12:15 tells us to "rejoice with those who rejoice and mourn with those who mourn". That is harder to do when others are rejoicing and you are mourning. A mature Christian grows to be able to do this.

I had to learn to refuse to stumble in faith over things the Lord did or didn't do; or things the Lord said or didn't say; or things the Lord did for others, but not for me.

The second verse that tested me and helped me grow at that time was verse 35. God is wise enough to do the right thing for every person in every situation. We must trust Him, at the same time recognising that His thoughts are not always the same as our thoughts and His ways are not always how we think He should act.

There is another principle I had to learn from John's experience, or more particularly from Jesus' silence in regard to John's personal situation: we must trust the character of God, no matter what. We must trust the Word of God and hold on to the revelation God has already given us, without the need for God to have to repeat Himself every time our faith gets shaky. The Lord does not have to keep telling us what we already know.

If there is a promise from God in His Word that fits our situation, then that is enough for us to believe for the miracle we need. God does not have to say or do any more. When we have faith in what God has already said and what Jesus has already done, we are ready for a miracle.

When we have faith in what God has already said and what Jesus has already done, we are ready for a miracle.

The only hitch is that we have to wait for the appointed time. That time will be when we have the faith equal to the answer we need. That is what happened to Abraham, as you can see in Romans 4:16-21. When he became "fully persuaded", his miracle came to pass. We are his faith-children. (Galatians 3:13-14, 29). We operate the same faith principles as Abraham did, but under a better covenant.

This same principle is found in Jesus' statement about receiving Holy Spirit. "If any man is thirsty, let him come to Me and drink. Whoever believes..." (John 7: 37-38). When you are thirsty, you are ready. Thirstiness signals God's time has come. Coming and drinking is belief; it is faith in action.

What is one thing you have learned from this teaching?

What is one thing you can do to implement this teaching?

Faith Declaration:

I thank You, Lord, that I can count on Your character, Word and wisdom, Your faithfulness, power and provision at all times in my life. I declare that I will trust You in good times and in tough times. I lean on Your Word and not my own understanding. I confess my faith in the promises of God and expect You to provide all I need to succeed, in Jesus' Name. Amen.

7 Get Godly Wisdom
and Make Good Decisions

The beginning of Wisdom is: get Wisdom (skillful and godly Wisdom)! [For skillful and godly Wisdom is the principal thing.] And with all you have gotten, get understanding (discernment, comprehension, and interpretation).
Proverbs 4:7 AMP

The King James version of this verse says: "*Wisdom is the principal thing.*"

The New Living Translation reads: "Getting wisdom is the wisest thing you can do!"

If you read Proverbs chapter 3, you will see the following benefits of having wisdom are listed:

(i)   Extended lifespan with peace and prosperity;

(ii) The Lord will direct and make straight and plain your paths. Always let Him lead you, and He will clear the road for you to follow. Seek His will in all you do and He will show you which path to take;

(iii) Health to your body and nourishment to your bones;

(iv) Riches and honour;

(v)   Pleasant ways, peace and blessing;

(vi) Safety and sweet sleep;

(vii) You will not be afraid of sudden disaster or ruin, for the LORD will be at your side and will keep your foot from being snared or stumbling.

Don't you want those benefits in your life? I'm sure you do, as I do. So, let's look at how we can increase in godly wisdom, which is defined in James 3:13–18.

7 Ways to get Godly Wisdom

(i) Cultivate the Fear of the Lord

> *Fear of the LORD is the foundation of wisdom. Knowledge of the Holy One results in good judgment...*
> *Proverbs 9:10 NLT*

> *The fool says in his heart, "There is no God."*
> *Psalm 14:1*

Wisdom starts when you fall in love with the Lord and choose a lifestyle of obeying God with a worshipful sense of adoration, awe, respect and submission.

> *A fool finds pleasure in doing mischief, wrong and evil conduct: but a man of understanding delights in wisdom; living wisely brings pleasure to the sensible.*
> *Proverbs 10:23*

Cultivating the fear of the Lord in your life is not just a spiritual thing; it is a commitment to a relationship with the Lord and to a lifestyle that pleases Him. We love Father God because He is so perfect, so good and so beautiful. We also admire, worship and obey Him because He is our Creator, our Lord and, one day, our Judge and our Rewarder.

> *If you are wise and understand God's ways, prove it by living an honorable life, doing good works with the humility that comes from wisdom.*

> *James 3:13 NLT*

When you are a believer who truly fears God in a worshipful way, you seek the Lord's Presence, His Heart and Mind and Hand and His Image in your life.

When you are a believer who truly fears God, you seek first the Kingdom of God, His Rulership in your life and His Purposes for you and for the world around you. You do this out of love and gratitude, not out of obligation or religious pressure.

> *When you are a believer who truly fears God, you can ask God to give you His Wisdom and He will. (James 1: 5-8).*

If you use His wisdom, if you practice what you preach, you will start reaping all the benefits Proverbs 3 talks about.

(ii) Position yourself to gain Knowledge and Understanding

Wisdom is gained by knowing facts and learning how they fit together to produce good outcomes.

> *A wise person is hungry for knowledge: but the fool feeds on stupidity and rubbish.*
> *Proverbs 15:14*

We do learn from God's Word. This is why He wrote it. His Word is full of instruction and godly wisdom for every life decision, especially the decision to get to know Him.

We don't learn only from textbooks or educational courses, we also learn from people who have succeeded in life. Even some who have failed can at least tell us, or help us discover, how they went wrong and we can learn from that.

The greatest teacher most of us learn wisdom from is experience; our own and other people's.

Get Godly Wisdom and Make Good Decisions

Simpletons only learn the hard way, but the wise learn by listening.

Proverbs 21:11 The Message

So, what is "experience"? It's not just an event. Experience is more to do with the life impact of that event and the personal growth that impact produces in us.

American comedian Will Rogers is credited with saying: "Good judgment comes from experience, and a lot of that comes from bad judgment."

That's a good explanation of what I mean regarding the personal growth that life's events and consequences produce in us. An experienced person has learned from and grown up through the school of hard knocks. In the process he has left behind the mistakes and pains of the past but taken with him the wisdom he has gained from both good and bad events in his life.

Let me give you a humourous piece of wisdom from an anonymous source who said it is useful to employ when you make a mistake: "If at first you don't succeed, cover your tracks so no-one finds out." Its sister saying is: "If at first you don't succeed, find someone or something to blame." I quickly add the reassurance to my readers that I do not advocate these philosophies. I include them only for your enjoyment.

Here are three more quotes that are also attributed to Will Rogers:

If stupidity got us into this mess, then why can't it get us out?

Never miss a good chance to shut up.

Live in such a way that you would not be ashamed to sell your parrot to the town gossip.

(iii) Surround yourself with people who can provide you with good counsel, including correction.

Lessons From My Dog

Wise Christians are accountable to others. They seek personal life change, as well as the up-skilling of their abilities and spiritual gifts.

> *Fools think their own way is right; but the wise listen to the advice of others.*
> *Proverbs 12:15*

> *Plans go wrong for lack of advice; many advisers bring success.*
> *Proverbs 15:22 NLT*

> *Without consultation, plans are frustrated, but with many counsellors they succeed.*
> *Proverbs 15:22 NAS*

(iv) Plan ahead

> *A prudent person foresees danger and takes precautions. The simpleton goes blindly on and suffers the consequences.*
> *Proverbs 22:3 and 27.12 NLT*

You have probably heard a saying similar to this: One teaspoon of prevention is better than a truckload of cure.

It happens to be true.

God Himself plans ahead. (Isaiah 25:1). Prophecy is a declaration of God's plan for the future. Jeremiah 29:11 tells us that He has good plans for us. The Lord has also planned, from even before we were born, what good works He intends for us to do in the life. God doesn't just act spontaneously. Jesus was born at the pre-arranged time, the appointed time or as Galatians 4:4 puts it in "the fullness of time".

When I was teaching at Wollongong University and the Gippsland Institute of Advanced Education, my students knew if I had prepared my lecture or tutorial or not. It was far more stressful for me to teach at that level if I went into the classroom unprepared and it was far less helpful to my students.

I know there are some ministers who can successfully preach spontaneously, and they might even say prophetically, on a regular basis. I can tell you that such preachers are few and far between and they are successful only because they are very knowledgeable of God's Word and very experienced in communicating His Truth. They have years of serious Bible study and of preparing messages behind them.

Too many people want to preach spontaneously and call it prophetic, because they are too lazy to prepare a decent meal for the people of God. They feed the Lord's people instant, ready-flavoured milk or someone else's revelation. I need to warn you that even when you are in the pulpit, under an anointing of Holy Spirit, you are not infallible. You can still say the wrong thing. It is more honouring to God, more beneficial to His people and safer for you, if you step up to speak with a prepared word from God. By all means let Holy Spirit tweak it while you are speaking, but don't presume that all you have to do to be a preacher is to open your mouth and He will fill it. That is twisting what the Psalmist (81:10) wrote to fit your own slackness.

(v)   Control yourself

> *God has not given us a spirit of fear, but of power, love and a sound mind, self-discipline and self-control*
> *2 Timothy 1:7*

What do you need to control in your life? Let me suggest a few specific areas: Your Mind, Emotions, Tongue, Sexuality, Stomach and your other appetites, Money, Actions and Reactions etc.

> *People with understanding control their anger: but a quick- and hot-tempered man shows great foolishness.*
> *Proverbs 14:29 (also 12.16 and 29.11)*

Lessons From My Dog

Let me give you two pieces of advice here:

Firstly, when something goes wrong or someone says something you do not like, take a deep breath, take some time to calm down and then respond to it. Don't react and, even more importantly, don't over-react to it. Pour water on the fire, not petrol.

Secondly, don't panic; stick to the game plan. As a Christian, that means sticking to God's game plan, which is the Word of God.

There are two Proverbs that the Lord has highlighted to me on a number of occasions over the years.

> *A person without self-control is like a city with broken-down walls.*
> *Proverbs 25:28 NLT*

A person who can't control himself, his tongue, his actions or reactions is vulnerable. He is easily overwhelmed by an enemy or out-manoeuvred by an opponent or manipulated by people.

I said a person who "can't" control himself, but I really meant "won't" control himself, because the Lord gives us self-control. So, saying you can't control yourself is a cop-out. You need to take responsibility for yourself. Then, you are more likely to act wisely and be victorious, prosperous and successful. You are more likely to gain the benefits of wisdom, because self-control is a sign of a mature and wise person.

> *Better a patient man than a warrior, a man who controls his temper than one who takes a city.*
> *Proverbs 16:32*

This verse tells us that the Lord ranks the development of our character higher than our achievements. So, developing Christ-like qualities such as self-control and wisdom will bring greater reward on that day when you stand before God.

Get Godly Wisdom and Make Good Decisions

(vi) Build good relationships and communication.

Learn how to and put the effort into being a good family member and a great team member or leader in every sphere of life and ministry.

> *He who walks with the wise grows wise; but a companion of fools gets into trouble and suffers harm.*
> *Proverbs 13:20*

> *Two people are better off than one, for they can help each other succeed.*
> *Ecclesiastes 4:9*

> *To answer before listening — that is folly and shame.*
> *Proverbs 18:13*

> *Don't use foul or abusive language. Let everything you say be good and helpful, so that your words will be an encouragement to those who hear them.*
> *Ephesians 4:29 NLT*

You need to develop good people and communication skills.

Some of these are:

(a) ability to encourage, empathise with, support, motivate and influence others

(b) building team identity, focus and action

(c) problem solving and conflict resolution

(d) listening

(e) understanding the importance of body language and tone of voice in communication;

(f)   speaking confidently and clearly;

(g)   talking to people and treating them in a friendly and respectful way;

(h)   showing interest and compassion

(i)   asking questions and letting people know that you believe what they have told you

(j)   keeping an open mind, not jumping to false conclusions or making foolish assumptions – remember: "to assume can make an ass out of you or me"

(k)   honesty, integrity, reliability, including following through on your promises;

(l)   exercising good and fair judgement in regard to both people and things

(m)   having a sense of humour. Generally speaking, smiling creates a great atmosphere for communication, whether in casting vision, setting out policy directives, negotiating or problem solving. Of course there are occasions when a smile or humour can be quite inappropriate and counter-productive

(n)   training, trusting and being patient with people.

(vii)   Be a good and generous manager and investor of the money and of the true riches that the Lord entrusts to you.

> *There is treasure to be desired and oil in the dwelling of the wise; but a foolish man wastefully spends all he has.*
> *Proverbs 21:20*

> *And he who had received the five talents came forward, bringing five talents more, saying, Master, you delivered to me five talents; here I have made five talents more.'* [21] *His master said to him, 'Well done, good and faithful servant. You have*

been faithful over a little; I will set you over much. Enter into the joy of your master.'
Matthew 25:20-21 ESV

Those words of Jesus: "*Well done, good and faithful servant*" are not automatically heard by every Christian when they go to Heaven. To hear them you must "do" good things ("well") with the resources of time, talents, treasure, testimonies, truth and spiritual gifts that the Lord gives you. You must be a "good" person and a "good" servant who is "faithful" to God and His Word and His Will both in terms of (a) reliable, consistent, persistent friendship and partnership with the Lord over the long haul; and (b) demonstrating a lifestyle of active faith, which is being "faith-full".

12 Ways to make Wise, Godly, Good Decisions

It's not enough to get wisdom. You actually have to use it. Sadly King Solomon, who is often credited with being the wisest man who ever lived, did not take his own advice. Many people make that same mistake.

If Solomon is the author of Ecclesiastes, you can see how disillusioned he became. He also disobeyed his own wisdom and the Lord's commands by taking foreign wives and allowing them to continue their idolatrous practices. He did not finish well as he should have.

Decisions are the big and small blocks on which lives, ministries, businesses and organisations are built. There are all kinds of decisions we have to make each day, ranging from the unimportant to the urgent and to the significant. In this chapter I am talking about serious decisions, the kind that make a difference in your life. Some of these decisions do not seem life-changing straight away, but over time they can surely make or break you.

The first drink you take doesn't seem to hurt much. However if you get drunk, you can get into huge trouble. If you become an alcoholic, your life will really fall apart on so many levels, such as your health, relationships, employment and finances. This illustrates the fact that if you consistently make wrong decisions, your life can go really haywire. Sadly, sometimes just one bad decision can have huge negative long-term consequences.

Most of us have heard the saying: "*Everything happens for a reason.*" The thing is that sometimes the reason is that the person has not acted in godly wisdom, but in worldly stupidity. Don't blame the results of bad judgments, foolish choices or wrong decisions on fate or karma (I don't believe in either of those concepts) or the devil (although he could have inspired the negative situation) or, worst of all, on God (Who never does anything wrong, unfair or foolish). If you think God is your problem, then you won't have faith for Him to be your solution.

Making right decisions builds your character, relationships and future. The best decisions that produce the most favourable results are those that are Biblical and Spirit-led.

> *He who deals wisely and heeds [God's] word and counsel shall find good, and whoever leans on, trusts in, and is confident in the Lord — happy, blessed, and fortunate is he.*
> *Proverbs 16:20 AMP*

(i) Have right motives, including wanting God's Will above all else.

(ii) Read your Bible to discern God's Will and to make sure your decision is scripturally wise and valid. Two biblical principles you can check your decisions against are these: will it glorify God and will it do good for others?

(iii) Get your mind and emotions under the control of Holy Spirit. Don't make decisions in a state of turmoil or in the heat of the moment when you are reacting to something that has happened.

(iv) Pray to and listen to the Lord. As you pray, you will realise that what is of God will grow stronger, more attractive and more exciting to your faith. What is not of God will get weaker and become less appealing. As you pray, ask for God's wisdom. (James 1:5-8).

(v) Ask yourself: What would be the common sense decision? What have you learned from your training, from past experience and from things you have seen happen in other people's lives? Think about what advice you would give someone else in the same situation.

(vi) Make sure that what you are deciding is morally, ethically and legally acceptable.

(vii) Listen to wise, godly people, especially your own family and pastor or church group leader. Recently, at a family dinner, I casually raised the subject of me buying a small motor bike. The whole family with one voice howled me down. So, that means no motor bike for me. Let me tell you another great wisdom principle: "Happy wife, happy life."

(viii) Check your inner feelings.

- Do you have peace within? (Colossians 3:15).
- Is your faith, excitement and joy rising or falling?
- Do you feel any inner negatives? Are you getting cold inside about the matter under consideration?
- Even if you have some fear that may not necessarily mean it is the wrong thing to decide or be involved with; it may indicate you are nervous about your ability to succeed. That's when you need faith.
- You will have faith if and when you are confident that what you are making decisions about is God's Will for your life.

(ix)   Is it in line with your life's purpose and giftedness?

(x)   Is the timing right?   Bishop Bill Hamon teaches that three things have to come into alignment before the fullness of what God wants to happen can be fulfilled. The three things are: God's Will, God's Way and God's When. You must know what God wants you to do. You must know how He intends for it to come to pass. You must be in sync with His calendar and timetable.

Here are some points to consider re timing:

(a) Is it for right now? Does God have or do you know you have to do some preliminary things before it is time for you to move forward? For example, do you need to improve your education or re-arrange your finances or other resources? You might need to get out of debt by downsizing your house.

(b) Ask the Lord for and wait until you get the confirmations you need for major decisions.

When my wife Lynne and I were considering moving interstate, we had every kind of confirmation, including Scriptures, inner witness, prophetic words and the alignment of circumstances. More recently, when I handed over my church to my associate pastor in order to focus on writing and inter-church and international ministry, I had the consensus of our local and denominational overseers, the inner witness and still, small voice of the Lord and some amazing prophetic confirmations. A visiting Indian prophet named the year of service I was in (my thirty-second. He literally saw the number 32) and the names of my two daughters. That was a miraculous confirmation of the timing of the Lord for our transition.

(c) Don't be rushed into making a decision you are not sure about.

(xi)   Ask yourself: Have I got the right partners, or the wrong ones?

Am I unequally yoked to unbelievers? (2 Corinthians 6:14). Do my partners have resources and skills that I need? Have I known my potential partners long enough to have built up trust based on their proven integrity and performance?

(xii) Can you see the Hand of God leading you in a certain direction? Are doors open or closed, opening or closing?

Use discernment to understand if God is with you or trying to stop you (as He did Balaam in Numbers 22:21-34); or, if the evil one is hindering you (as he did Paul in 1 Thessalonians 2:18); or, if people are pressuring you to do their will, not God's; or, if you are simply being selfish.

You must resist the devil and press on, knowing the Lord is with you to help you overcome every obstacle and succeed in the mission He has appointed you to fulfil. Don't expect the enemy to flee from you in the first round of every battle. (James 4:7).

Sometimes we try to convince ourselves that a decision is the Lord's Will, just because we want to do it. That is how many Christians take the Lord's Name in vain. They say the Lord told me to do this or that, when He didn't.

What is one thing you have learned from this teaching?

___

What is one thing you can do to implement this teaching?

___

Faith Declaration:

Lord I thank You for Your Word and Your Holy Spirit living in me and the wisdom of God You make available and known to me. I put myself, my mind, my relationships and partnerships and my decisions fully into Your Hands. I ask You to guide me into Your perfect will in every area of my life. I declare the riches of Your grace are coming to me as I make Spirit-led decisions that attract Your favour and Divine Partnership. I confess success and prosperity and all the benefits of operating with the wisdom of God are mine, in Jesus Name. Amen.

8   3 Kinds of Forgiveness

Be kind and compassionate to one another, forgiving each other, just as in Christ God forgave you.
Ephesians 4:32

Throughout history there have been amazing examples of forgiveness.

- God forgave Paul, who called himself "the worst of sinners" in 1 Timothy 1:15-16. The Bible says that without Christ, we were not only sinners, but God's enemies. (Romans 5:8-10).

- On Tuesday 27 January 2015, the online *Daily Mail* Australia ran an article headed: "Could you forgive your rapist, your father for murdering your mother or a drunk driver for killing your husband? These brave women did..." It went on to share the stories of the four women, including Joanne Nodding and Natalia Aggiano, who were involved in those terrible real-life incidents.

- Uchendi Nwani was the stepson of a prominent Baptist pastor in Nashville. He lived a double life as a serious drug dealer while still at school. After he was arrested and served time in jail, Uchendi came out of prison carrying his Bible, with the goal of making his parents proud. He is now a multi-millionaire barber-school owner, who has helped many at-risk youth and supported church prison programmes.

These examples illustrate the three kinds of forgiveness we all need to implement in our lives.

Lessons From My Dog

(i)   Receiving forgiveness from God for our sins.

It is important to understand that we never forgive God for anything, because He is perfect and never does any wrong. No matter what we think God should have done or not done or stopped from happening, He is infinitely good, wise and holy. He never makes mistakes. He always has our best interests at heart, because He is motivated by the highest form of love that is possible to experience and express, the (Greek) "agape" love of God.

> *The Rock! His work is perfect, for all His ways are just; a God of faithfulness and without injustice, righteous and upright is He.*
>
> *Deuteronomy 32:4 NAS*

The second important matter to understand is that we do not just confess our sins once when we get saved and never again. I am shocked by people who teach an error concerning the fact that the sacrifice and triumph of Jesus was for all sin, for all people, for all time.

Their error is that they say all our sins past, present and future were washed away by the Blood of Jesus on the cross. Therefore, we do not need to confess our sins other than when we first get saved, because they are all forgiven.

Let me illustrate what I believe: Imagine you won a year's supply of groceries. You go to the store to collect your prize. You take everything you want. The next day you realise that in your excitement, as you selected so many treats you normally would have not taken, you forgot a couple of essential things. Will the items somehow self-deliver themselves to your door? No, they won't. Do you have to go back to the store to get what you didn't take the first trip? Yes, you will have to go back to the store and explain to the people that you didn't take all to which you were entitled.

Similarly, when we get saved, we ask the Lord to forgive all the sins we have committed up to that point in our lives. How can we ask Him to forgive sins we haven't committed, sins we don't even know that we will commit? The fact is that we do need to confess our future sins, but only at the time we commit them, or after, definitely not before.

Even though the Lord does know in advance that we will commit our future sins and He has provided for our forgiveness, we cannot ask for forgiveness of something that hasn't happened.

We can only confess and be forgiven of sins we have already committed. Therefore after we are saved, we must continue to repent of and ask forgiveness for sins we commit in the course of our life.

In John 13:1-17, Jesus taught the apostles to let Him wash their feet.

> *Jesus replied, "A person who has bathed all over does not need to wash, except for the feet, to be entirely clean.*
> *John 13:10*

The spiritual meaning of this verse is that after you are saved (bathed), you need only to deal with the daily impact of the dirt of this world on your life. So, let's take the advice of the apostle John who was there that night with Jesus.

> *If we claim to be without sin, we deceive ourselves and the truth is not in us. ⁹ If we confess our sins, He is faithful and just and will forgive us our sins and purify us from all unrighteousness.*
> *1 John 1:8-9*

(ii)   The second kind of forgiveness is us forgiving others who have hurt or offended us.

It is impossible to go through life without experiencing hurts, wounds and disappointments. Some people's responses to these lead to depression, unforgiveness, breakdown of relationships, resentment and bitterness.

Jesus challenges and empowers us to love our critics, wrong-doers and even our enemies. (Luke 6:27-36).

Forgiving those who offend us is never easy, but it is a choice we can, should and indeed we must make. The New Testament makes it clear that, if we do not forgive others, then God will not forgive us. (Matthew 6:14–15).

The Lord always gives us the ability, by His Holy Spirit, to live according to His Word and example.

Without forgiving others, you will not be healed of the soul damage and the inner negatives of hurt, anger, resentment, bitterness or prejudice that offences inflict upon us.

Without forgiving others, you will not be healed of the soul damage and the inner negatives of hurt, anger, resentment, bitterness or prejudice that offences inflict upon us.

With forgiveness, there must also be the refusal to remember (or discuss) the offence any more. Keeping it alive in your memory, or in your mouth, keeps the pain alive in your soul.

The source of this quote is unknown, but I agree with its principles. "The first to apologise is the bravest. The first to forgive is the strongest. And the first to forget is the happiest."

(iii) The third area of forgiveness is that of forgiving ourselves.

There is therefore now no condemnation for those who are in Christ Jesus.
Romans 8:1

We can learn from our mistakes. We can do better next time. We need to give ourselves time to heal. There is a time gap between when you forgive yourself (and others) by faith and when your emotions catch up with your faith.

We have to do the same as the Lord does with our sins. We have to choose to not remember them anymore.

Possibly the greatest examples of this are the apostles Peter and Paul, Mary Magdalene and the woman of Samaria. They all had much about which to forgive themselves.

Every time Peter heard a rooster crow after Jesus' death must have reminded him of his sin of denying his Lord and friend. Yet Peter was able to move forward with his life and ministry without carrying the baggage of lingering guilt or shame or regret.

Paul was also able to leave his negative past behind, even though he described himself as the worst of sinners. (1 Timothy 1:15; Philippians 3:12-14).

Mary Magdalene had seven demons. What sinful, even Satanic, things had she experienced that had brought her into such captivity of the devil? Yet she was so close to the Lord, because she lived in the freedom of His forgiveness and healing.

The woman of Samaria had five husbands and a de-facto. What a walking relationship disaster she was. I believe she was sexually abused as a child. Thereafter, she allowed men to use and mistreat her.

She was so ashamed of her past and present and so conscious of the judgement of her fellow villagers that she went to the well in the heat of the day to avoid the rejection and scorn of her peers. She refused to go at the same time as they went to the well. It's possible that she could have been shunned not only because of the unacceptability of her defacto relationship in the culture of that day, but also because other women did not trust her to get to know their husbands.

After Jesus came into her life, she turned into an instant evangelist, shouting His praises to all of her neighbours. She was able to forgive the men, her critics and herself and move into a ministry of influence. Hallelujah. What a mighty Saviour and Lord we have.

Don't keep focussing on your past mistakes, even if the latest one was only yesterday or an hour ago. Put it under the Blood. Fix it in whatever way you can.

Receive your forgiveness and healing. Move on. Don't keep beating yourself up because, when you do, you are doing the devil's job for him. When he comes to accuse you send him packing in Jesus' Name.

Don't do the devil's work by condemning yourself. When he accuses you, send him packing in Jesus' Name.

> *¹⁰ Then I heard a loud voice in heaven say: "Now have come the salvation and the power and the kingdom of our God, and the authority of his Messiah. For the accuser of our brothers and sisters, who accuses them before our God day and night, has been hurled down. ¹¹ They triumphed over him by the blood of the Lamb and by the word of their testimony; they did not love their lives so much as to shrink from death.*
>
> *Revelation 12:11*

To overcome the devil's accusations you must first accept that your sins are indeed washed away by the Blood of the Lamb. Just as the Lord does not remember our sins any more (Isaiah 43:25), we have to choose to accept our forgiveness and do the same as Him. This does not require us to get a case of amnesia, because God surely doesn't have amnesia. He simply chooses to put the sins He has forgiven out of His mind. That's what you need to do. Every time the memory of the sin comes into your mind, replace it with thoughts of something else. Rebuke it as coming from the devil, the accuser. Don't think of the accusation as coming from yourself and certainly not from God, because He has put it out of His Mind.

Secondly, speak out loud the word of your testimony that you are a saint, not a sinner; that you have been saved by grace; that your sins are under the Blood; that you are forgiven; that you are the righteousness of God in Christ. Amen.

Submit yourselves, then, to God. Resist the devil, and he will flee from you.
James 4:7

In order to overcome the accusations of the devil, you have to do two things. Firstly, submit to what God in His Word says about you. Remember this: You cannot resist both God and the devil at the same time. If you try to do that, you will be in a situation as if the walls are closing in on you from both sides. When you submit to God, you and He are now on the same side, pushing in the same direction against the devil and against sin, shame, guilt, sickness, depression and every evil thing. Secondly, resist the devil with the Word of God and in every spiritual way until he flees from you. Be aware that he is not likely to run away after only one skirmish.

Thirdly, understand what "loving not" your life is all about and do that. It does not mean (a) not living your full life span; or (b) not enjoying your life. It is about losing your life in the service of your Saviour and King, Jesus. That is ultimate satisfaction. You overcome condemnation by faith in what the Word of God says about you and by active faith in the form of doing the good works He prepared in advance for you to do. (Ephesians 2:10).

What is one thing you have learned from this teaching?

What is one thing you can do to implement this teaching?

Faith Declaration

I thank You Lord because You, Who are so perfectly holy, have forgiven me and clothed me with the righteousness of God in Christ. I am grateful that You have forgiven me all my sins, big and small, no matter how many of them there were. I praise You for the fact that Jesus has taken my punishment for my sins and enables me, by Your Word and Spirit, to break the power of sin in my life. I thank You for helping me forgive others and be healed of the hurts I felt and the bad attitudes I developed because of what happened. I declare in Jesus' Name that I am forgiven, healed and set free from my own feelings of guilt, shame, anger and depression. I praise You because You have enabled me to overcome the accusations and condemnation of the devil and criticisms of people. I rejoice in You, because You enable me to walk forward in my life with You, cleansed from and free of all my previous sins, in Jesus' Name. Amen. Hallelujah.

9 Faith

What is Faith? It is the confident assurance that something we want is going to happen. It is the certainty that what we hope for is waiting for us even though we cannot see it up ahead.
Hebrews 11:1 Living Bible

Now faith is the assurance (the confirmation, the title deed) of the things [we] hope for, being the proof of things [we] do not see and the conviction of their reality [faith perceiving as real fact what is not revealed to the senses].
Hebrews 11:1 AMP

Only Faith can guarantee the blessings we hope for or prove the existence of realities that at present remain unseen.
Hebrews 11:1 Jerusalem Bible

Saint Augustine said: "Faith is to believe what we do not see; and the reward of this faith is to see what we believe." He must have read Mark 11:22-24.

During a time of severe drought, a church called an emergency prayer meeting to pray for rain. The ones who had real faith brought an umbrella with them.

What is Faith?

- Faith is a confident expectation of God's promises coming to pass.

- Faith is being assured that the things we expect, due to what the Lord has said, will indeed happen.

- Faith is being convinced about things that have not happened yet, and therefore remain unseen.

(i) F-aith is:

Founded on God, meaning, on His nature and abilities.

When a person truly believes that God is the all-powerful, always-good and grace-giving Lord Who willingly and abundantly provides for our every need and righteous desire, then all things become possible.

A man walked too near the edge of a cliff. As he fell, he grabbed hold of a branch and held on for dear life. Every time he heard any kind of sound, he would call out: "Help, is there anybody up there?" For a long while no-one replied, because the sounds he heard were just the wind blowing the branches, small stones and other loose things on the cliff top. Finally, the man heard a Voice call back: "It's going to be OK. I am God. Trust Me and let go of the branch and I will save you." After a time of thinking about what the Voice said, the man cried out: "Is there anybody else up there?"

That man did not trust the Nature or Voice or Ability of God.

(ii) f-A-ith is:

Active confidence in God and His Word.

Christian Faith is not just accepting that the Bible is true. It is acting in accordance with what the Bible says. Some time ago, Holy Spirit said to me: When you do what the Bible says, God will do what the Bible says.

When you do what the Bible says, God will do what the Bible says

Faith is Active:

The just shall live by faith
Romans 1.17

Christians live according to Biblical principles every day of their lives. They trust in and rely on God in every area of life.

Faith without works is dead
James 2:17

Faith is knowing the will of God and doing it.

Faith is hearing the voice of God and obeying it.

True Christians are fully obedient to God, His Word and His Spirit. They do this willingly and cheerfully, because they love the Lord, not because of a sense of legalistic or religious duty.

Faith is Active Confidence:

Our faith makes possible all that is possible with God. (Mark 9.23; Matthew 19.26).

Believers expect God to answer prayer and fulfil the promises of His Word.

Evangelist, author and speaker Kevin Dedmon preached in our church. He expressed his faith, expectancy and confidence in God during one of his messages by saying: "When I pray, God comes and does good things."

I have a plaque on my desk that says: "Faith is not believing God can – it is knowing that He will."

Believers expect God to be willing to do good and great things.

The incident of Jesus telling the leper He was willing to heal him and then doing the miracle the man requested, was inserted into the Bible by Holy Spirit in order to teach us how willing God is!

Lessons From My Dog

(iii) fa-I-th is:

being In love with and In touch with the Lord.

We learn to put our faith in God by building an intimate, personal, daily relationship with Him.

We are King's kids, the adopted sons and daughters of God. Our sonship is the source of our blessing, inheritance and authority in Christ.

Think about this: If the father said yes to his rebellious, self-centred prodigal son, how much more will God our Heavenly Father say yes to you who want to please Him? Matthew and Luke both tell us that our Heavenly Father wants to bless His children "much more" than good, earthly fathers do. (Matthew 7.11; Luke 11.13).

> *... people who know their God will be strong and take action.*
> *Daniel 11:32b ISV*

The Hebrew word for "know" in this verse indicates intimate knowledge. When a Christian knows the Lord intimately, he becomes strong in the Lord and in the power of His might. His faith grows strong and he takes faith actions that lead to great exploits happening that bring glory to God and victory and blessing to His people.

(iv) fai-T-h is:

Total trust, as a little child in her perfect heavenly Father.

If you've ever seen a puppy roll over on her back for a tummy rub, then you have seen a picture of total trust and complete, willing, loving vulnerability.

We are to trust God even when our mind just does not and even cannot understand what is going on or why certain things are not happening.

> *Trust in the Lord with all your heart and lean not on your own understanding.*
> *Proverbs 3:5*

There are times when we must simply be still and know that He is God (Ps. 46:10a), because there's nothing else we can do.

These are times when we truly must walk by faith and not by sight. (2 Corinthians 5:7).

The key to total trust in God is to know beyond any shadow of a doubt that God is good and great all the time; that He is always with you and for you, not against you; and that the Lord will never hurt you, leave you, fail you, nor forget you.

(v) Fait-H is:

Holding on to God and His Word, no matter what, nor how long it takes for your miracle to become a reality in our material world. Remember, if you have claimed your miracle, your blessing, your inheritance by faith, based on the promises of God's Word, then, it already is a reality in the spiritual world of the Kingdom of God.

The Lord told Joshua He had already given the Promised Land to the new leader of Israel. But Joshua and the Jews still had to possess the land in order to make real on earth what God said was already real in His spiritual kingdom.

Hebrews 6:12b tells us that faith and patience, which are known in a more active form of expression as "persistence", are often both required in order to inherit the promises of God.

> *You need to persevere so that when you have done the will of God, you will receive what He has promised.*
> *Hebrews 10:36*

Years ago, Holy Spirit taught me that persistence overcomes enemy resistance. So keep on believing. Keep on doing what God wants you to do and the devil will not be able to rob you of your due season harvest or your appointed time miracle.

Be steadfast in prayer, understanding that faith is Forwarding All Items To Heaven. Jesus Himself said: Everyone who asks, receives. (Matthew 7:8a).

Lessons From My Dog

Don't just pray in a religious, casual, half-hearted way. The words "ask" and "receive" in Greek are strong, not weak, words.

Prayer is asking with conviction, based on the knowledge that the covenant has been fully paid for by Jesus. Therefore, the benefits of the covenant are a done deal.

The word Jesus used for "receive" is a military word that means "seize" the answer. We don't pray and passively wait for the answer for years. We sow into the answer, the harvest, by practical active faith. We take the opportunities that come our way and we create our own. We position ourselves to receive a miracle and to be a miracle

What is one thing you have learned from this teaching?

What is one thing you can do to implement this teaching

Faith Declaration

Lord I praise You because You are good and great. I thank You for rewarding my active faith. I declare that by Your grace my miracle will soon be manifest. I receive it by faith and speak it into being in Jesus' mighty Name. Amen. I thank You Lord for Your love for me. I know You always want what is best for me. I bring every thought of mine captive to the obedience of Christ and of Your Word. I declare my complete trust in You for my every need, godly desire and faith goal. I believe every resource, blessing and miracle will be manifest in my life soon, because Jesus has said "Yes" to every Bible promise. I now say the "Amen" in His Name. I declare that my faith, patience and persistence will be richly rewarded, because God's Word is true and Jesus is Lord. Amen.

10 You can be Strong

I can do all things through Christ Who strengthens me
Philippians 4:13

As you drive through a street you don't see much. How would you score if I pulled you over and asked you questions such as: "How many houses had red roofs? How many white fences did you see? Were there any dogs in the front yard? Which house had the biggest street number nailed on their fence?"

If you are like every other truthful driver, you would most likely say: "I think I would fail that test."

It's the same with the Bible. If you speed read your way through it, not much is going to sink in and you are going to miss some beautiful things that were there to inspire you.

I believe a close look at this one verse will prove this to you.

Before I focus on its specifics, let me say that you should bring your Bible to church and a pen so you can take notes. When you read your Bible at home or at work alone or on the train, write the thoughts you have about what you are reading in a notebook or even in your Bible itself.

Yes, I do mean scribble in your Bible.

On the other hand you can do as I do and take notes on your smartphone. It doubles as a Bible reader but I prefer to take a paper Bible with me.

Why don't you stop reading and stir your faith right now by saying out loud: "I can do all things through Christ Who strengthens me."

(i) "I"

I want you to notice something about this verse – it is written in the singular, like Psalm 23. This verse is about each Christian's personal responsibility to partner with Jesus in his or her own life.

It is not written like the Our Father prayer Jesus taught His disciples, which is all plural. Jesus used all plurals to teach His disciples that believers should never pray selfish or self-centred prayers. We should always pray for others as well.

Holy Spirit's use of the singular pronouns in Philippians 4:13 tells us that each person must put his faith in the Lord to give him strength and victory. You can and you must trust the Lord Jesus to help you, in every area of life.

The "I" in this verse means that Christ will strengthen any and every Christian, without exceptions. That means you qualify for the Lord's help. Just put your name and your faith in this verse and Jesus will begin to give you His strength. Hallelujah.

(ii) "I Can"

Christians must be positive people. You cannot have a negative mind and mouth and also say you have faith in God.

You cannot have a negative mind and mouth and also say you have faith in God.

Don't say "I can't", when God says "you can."

In your strength I can crush an army; I can run through a barricade; with my God I can scale any wall.

Psalm 18:29

Faith is real when you believe and act upon the principles and promises of God's Word. So by faith, act as if you can, not as if you can't.

(iii) "Do"

The Bible says faith without works or actions is dead. So, I must act by faith, in accordance with God's Word.

If I feel afraid, I will act courageously because the Bible says "*God has not given me a spirit of fear.*" (2 Timothy 1:7).

If I need healing I will believe God to touch me with His power and demonstrate this by speaking out loud the Scriptures about healing and commanding my body to conform to the Word of God.

If my finances are tight, I faithfully and faith-fully implement Biblical economics by giving to God, sowing before I reap, acting wisely with my spending and working hard as unto the Lord. My active faith will trigger the Lord's help. I have heard plenty of testimonies over the years from Christians who have said at the end of a lean period: "The Lord got us through and provided for us every step along the way." I say Amen to that for myself and my family. Jehovah Jireh has brought us through every test and provided for us to not merely survive, but to be blessed in order to bless others.

Philippians 4:13 tells me that: I am the doer and Jesus is my power supply.

One of the greatest principles of faith in the Word of God is what the Lord said to Gideon.

Then the LORD turned to him and said, "Go with the strength you have, and rescue Israel from the Midianites. I am ending you!"

Judges 6:14

Don't wait until you have more strength or most likely until you "feel" you have more strength. Use the faith and the strength you already have. When you use what you've already got, Jesus will add His strength to it and you will triumph as Gideon did.

Here is another way to use your faith to plug into the strength of the Lord.

> *...Let the weak say, 'I am strong.'*
> *Joel 3:10b NKJV*

(iv) "All things"

Are these two words to be taken absolutely literally? No.

This verse does not mean a Christian can cook food without fire or fuel or power. It does not mean we can speak a foreign language without ever having learned it ... although I have heard of very rare miracles where this has happened.

Philippians 4:13 actually means that, through Christ, I can do all things that are God's Will for my life. Through Christ, I can do all the things God wants me to do.

- I can be a good father or mother
- I can be a good son or daughter
- I can be a good student
- I can be a good worker
- I can be a good minister for the glory of God
- I can be a good cook
- I can be a good on the computer
- I can be a good helper
- I can be a good example to others

- I can be a good leader
- I can be good in business
- I can be a good giver
- What do you need to be good at? Put it in here! "I can be a good …."

God gives us the strength, resources and blessing to do all the things that He has willed for our lives.

You have probably heard the saying: "God's Will is God's bill." That is not just about money. It includes every resource you need to succeed in every area of life and ministry.

(v) "Through Christ"

The Greek word used here literally means "in Christ."

This tells us that we are not alone and we are not restricted to our human resources or limitations. We have a wonderful and powerful Partner, the Lord Jesus Christ Himself.

> *For out of His fullness (abundance) we have all received [all had a share and we were all supplied with] one grace after another and spiritual blessing upon spiritual blessing and even favour upon favour and gift [heaped] upon gift.*
> *John 1:16 AMP*

> *May you experience the love of Christ, though it is too great to understand fully. Then you will be made complete with all the fullness of life and power that comes from God.*
> *Ephesians 3:19 NLT*

Why don't you stop reading and say out loud right now: I am the doer and Jesus is my power supply.

You Can Be Strong

Now speak out loud the Amplified Bible's version of Philippians 4:13.

> *I have strength for all things in Christ Who empowers me [I am ready for anything and equal to anything through Him Who infuses inner strength into me; I am self-sufficient in Christ's sufficiency].*

When you truly believe that Jesus really is in your life and you are truly in His, then all things will be possible to you.

Let's remind ourselves of the fact that Jesus lives within.

Right now, put your hand out in front of you as if you were about to shake another person's hand in greeting.

Because Jesus lives inside you, when you put out your hand, then He puts out His hand.

You are the Hands of Jesus now.

And that's not all.

- When Jesus wants to talk to someone He talks through you.
- When Jesus wants to touch someone He touches them through you.
- When Jesus wants to go somewhere, He goes there through you.
- When Jesus wants to love someone, He loves them through you.
- When Jesus wants to help someone, He helps them through you.

Our strength is not in ourselves, our personality, our talents, or our abilities. Our strength is not even our anointings or spiritual gifts. Our strength in our relationship with Jesus Christ, Who strengthens us.

> *Not that we are fit (qualified and sufficient in ability) of ourselves ……., but our power and ability and sufficiency are from God.*
> *2 Corinthians 3:5 AMP*

(vi) "Strengthens"

I want you to notice that the word "strengthens" is in the present tense. It signifies that the Lord Jesus, Who is in you, is strengthening you in the very moment that you need His strength. In fact, Christ is continually strengthening you. You just need to be aware of His constant infilling and receive it by faith.

The present tense indicates that Jesus is continually able to pour in to us the power we need to succeed each and every day and moment. That continuing strength comes from a limitless Source. It flows into our lives, as we walk by faith in Christ and with Christ.

So, if we experience a "power shortage" or "power failure", it is not because of a failure in the supply from the Source. It is because of a failure to depend on and draw from the Source, by faith.

Any lack of strength is not because of a problem with Jesus the power-Supplier. We simply must learn how to draw from Him, our Source, by faith.

If you are about to do something difficult, say in your heart: "Lord, I draw on Your strength right now. I confess that I can do this because You are strengthening me in the here and now of my life. Amen."

(vii) "Me"

In English, Philippians 4:13 finishes with the same person it began with, namely, me.

There is a well-known saying: If it is to be – it's up to me

This verse tells each and everyone of us that we as individual believers must be in partnership with Jesus in order to have the strength to fulfil all the things that the Lord has planned for us.

I cannot depend on or blame others. God plus me is enough to fulfil my potential and destiny. He will gather around me and unto me all the resources of people, money, things, opportunities, anointings, natural and spiritual gifts I need to succeed .... if I believe ... and if I act on what I believe about God and His Word.

If and when I become the doer, then Jesus will surely be my power-Supplier.

> *Even so faith, if it has no works, is dead ...*
> *James 2:17 NAS*

Here is a summary of what primary issues this verse addresses:

"I can" is about my Attitude, my Philosophy of life and ministry.

"Do" refers to my Actions, my Personal sense of responsibility.

"All Things" covers my Assignment, my Purpose.

"Through" and "in" Christ describes my Anointing, my Power-source.

"Strengthens" focusses on my Ability, my Potential in life and ministry.

Let's end this chapter with faith and gratitude by saying this verse out loud. But this time, I want you to say it three times and insert your own name as you do:

- I (your name here) can do all things through Christ Who strengthens me. Hallelujah.
- I (your name here) can do all things through Christ Who strengthens me. Hallelujah.
- I (your name here) can do all things through Christ Who strengthens me. Hallelujah.

Lessons From My Dog

What is one thing you have learned from this teaching?

_____

What is one thing you can do to implement this teaching?

_____

Faith Declaration:

I thank You Lord for strengthening me when I step out in faith. I praise you because Your Partnership in my life makes all things possible. I declare in Jesus' Name that I am not weak and I do not lack whatever it takes to succeed. I decree that I have strength for today, I have strength for every day, I have strength for every task, every situation and every opportunity, in Jesus' Name. Amen.

11   God Who balances the scales

A false balance is an abomination to the LORD, but a just weight is His delight.
Proverbs 11:1 NAS

The LORD detests double standards; He is not pleased by dishonest scales.
Proverbs 20:23

When we think of these verses in terms of life and not in a commercial context, we can see that the Lord is not pleased if our lives are out of balance. In this chapter, we learn from the prayer of Moses in Psalm 90 that we can ask and expect God to help us overcome life situations in which there is too much negativity and not enough good. The kingdom of God is not characterized by never-ending temptations, trials and tests, but by righteousness, peace and joy in and by the grace of God administered to us by Holy Spirit. (Romans 14:17).

Give us gladness in proportion to our former misery! Replace the evil years with good.
Psalm 90:15

We all love a story about someone's rags-to-riches success, like that of Susan Boyle, runner-up on *"Britain's Got Talent"* in 2009.

Lessons From My Dog

We praise God for the testimony of a person who bounces back from adversity, like Bethany Hamilton. At the age of 13, she could have died when a shark attacked her. She lost her left arm. Her faith in God and personal determination were so strong that two years later she won first place in the Explorer Women's division of the USA National Scholastic Surfing Association Championships. Her story is told in the 2011 movie *"Soul Surfer"*. She certainly exemplifies the fact that having faith in God, Who balances the scales, will bring amazing turnarounds in your life.

Let's look at the second part of the little-known, but very encouraging, Psalm 90 verse by verse.

> [12] *Teach us to realise the brevity of life, so that we may grow in wisdom.*

Life has a way of seemingly slipping through our fingers. Children grow up so fast. I think our culture causes our children to grow up too fast. Parents should make sure their children are not being exposed to knowledge and experiences that they are not mature enough to process positively.

Understanding that life is brief, like a fog that lifts and dissipates quickly after it has formed (refer James 4:14), is an important motivator to living a focussed, purposeful life. That is one way a person can live a wise life. They will make the best they can of the life they have.

The greatest priority that should be evoked by understanding how brief is our earthly life, is that we live with eternity in mind. That means living God's way, not man's way, not our own way. It means living for His glory and His reward, not for the glory of man, or self, or the rewards of this worldly life. This is one of the meanings of Proverbs 9:10 which says: *"the fear of the Lord is the beginning of wisdom."*

When you live with eternity as your focus, you understand that there will be a day of judgement for each and every human being, on the day of the Lord's choosing. That's a good reason to live wisely, meaning with godly wisdom. It's a good reason to live a life based on the Bible and to make Jesus your Saviour and Lord.

God Who Balances the Scales

Another aspect to realising the brevity of life is to understand that if your life is to turn around, as this prayer is asking God to do, you must learn from the mistakes of the past. Don't waste time living in the past. Don't let the past imprison you.

> *¹³ O LORD, come back to us! How long will You delay? Take pity on Your servants!*

If you want your life to turn around, you must get right with God. Imagine having a shirt with a full row of buttons down the front. If you get the first button wrong, then every other button is out of sync and you look completely out of order. That's what life is like when you don't put God first in your life. Your life is not in the order or balance God desires. This will frustrate both you and the Lord, either in the short or long term or both.

The Great Shepherd Psalm (23) promises that goodness and mercy will follow those who follow Jesus, like good sheep of His pasture. If they don't follow Him, this and all the other promises of that extraordinary Psalm do not apply. Moses' prayer recognises that a person must be in good relationship with God if they want their life to be better than it has been.

> *¹⁴ Satisfy us each morning with your unfailing love, so we may sing for joy to the end of our lives.*

Knowing the love of God in a personal way has tremendous comforting, healing, uplifting and esteem-building side-effects. In the otherwise quite miserable book of Lamentations there is a bright, shining jewel of light and hope:

> *²² The faithful love of the Lord never ends! His mercies never cease. ²³ Great is His faithfulness; His mercies begin afresh each morning. ²⁴ I say to myself, "The Lord is my inheritance; therefore, I will hope in Him!"*
>
> Lamentations 3:22-24 NLT

Lessons From My Dog

This tells us that no matter how dark, lonely or depressing your life might be at this time, God can always touch you with His love, refresh you with His mercy and give you hope for the future. The Lord is your inheritance. God has a rich inheritance of all the promises in His Word for you to experience and enjoy.

His new mercy, new grace, new love, new blessing, new hope, new peace and new power are yours for the taking, by faith, each and every day. Whether you had a good day or a bad one yesterday or the day before or for however long, you can start each new day believing for a better day today. When you believe, you will receive the resources you need from the Lord to achieve success.

You can start each new day believing for a better day today. When you believe, you will receive the resources you need from the Lord to achieve success.

---

[15] Give us gladness in proportion to our former misery! Replace the evil years with good.

This is the big thing for which you can hope. This is what you can believe God will do for you. If you can have this kind of faith in the God Who balances the scales of your life, then you can experience the reverse of what Egypt did. Based on the interpretation of Pharoah's dreams, Joseph predicted that seven good years of prosperity would be followed by seven years of drought leading to an international famine.

This prayer believes for the Lord to put His hand of favour, blessing, provision and power on your life for years to come. This will well and truly reverse the curse of sin and Satanic opposition and fleshly stupidity that have depleted your life.

God Who Balances the Scales

¹⁶ Let us, your servants, see You work again; let our children see Your glory.

Now Moses prays for the evident power and glory of God to be revealed to His people and their families. What a magnificent experience it is to have a Divine encounter with the manifest presence of God. How marvellous it is when God Himself "shows up" in worship or empowers a person to get out of their wheelchair completely healed and able to live a normal life again. This is what Moses is encouraging us to pray for.

Yes, God is omnipresent. He is present everywhere, all the time. However, we humans do not see Him or feel Him everywhere, all the time. We know He is there by faith. We know He is there, with us, as God, the Omnipresent, Omniscient, Omnipotent covenant-keeping Senior Partner of His people. The Book of Esther testifies that God still does supernatural things while remaining invisible. It also teaches us that God is at work even we don't realise it or see anything happening.

The Book of Esther testifies that God still does supernatural things while remaining invisible. It also teaches us that God is at work even we don't realise it or see anything happening.

When the Lord chooses to reveal Himself in an obvious way, it is a special moment indeed. This is what we want our families to experience. This is what makes God so very real and personal to them as individuals. This is why it is so rare for people saved during a genuine revival to ever waiver in their faith. It's because they have had a personal encounter with the Living God. Hallelujah. `

I think it is fair to say that God has been revealing Himself more and more in recent decades, through visions, dreams and manifestations of His supernatural knowledge and power. There also seem to be far more revelations of angels in an ongoing fulfilment of what Jesus said to Nathaniel in John 1:51.

Lessons From My Dog

> *¹⁷ And may the Lord our God show us his approval and make our efforts successful. Yes, make our efforts successful!*

Now Moses demonstrates the requirement for our active faith, not just faith in prayer. God does not just do things for us. He works with us to make our works of love, faith and obedience successful. You can be sure that when the Lord is truly your personal Senior Partner, He will make your efforts successful as He did for Joseph and David in the Old Testament. (Genesis 39:2-3; 1 Samuel 18:14).

We receive all things the same way we receive salvation. Ephesians 2:8 tells us that we are saved by grace through faith. Every good thing we get from God is because of His unconditional generosity toward His children. However, receiving what God gives requires our obedient, active faith.

> *Keep on asking, and you will receive what you ask for.*
> *Matthew 7:7 NLT*

When Jesus made this statement He used two strong words. When you study the word Jesus used for "ask", you discover that it has the implicit meaning of putting a demand on the grace of God based on a covenant, the requirements of which have been met. Of course, He said this before He met those requirements; but because of Calvary, the new covenant has been sealed and activated by Jesus' sacrifice and triumph.

The word Jesus used for "receive" is the Greek word "lambano". This is another strong word. It has military connotations, because it means to "seize". So, receiving is not a passive thing. Some Christians think that, if they pray sometimes and go to church occasionally and even read their Bibles every now and then, God should shower them with blessings while they are watching television or when they are in need.

Jesus used a strong word for "receive". "Lambano" means to "seize". Receiving is not a passive thing.

God Who Balances the Scales

The reality is that God responds more to faith than He does to need. Hebrews 11:6 says the Lord rewards those who *"earnestly seek Him."* (NIV). Those who receive blessings and miracles the "lambano" way are those who put their faith on the line consistently, as a lifestyle and specifically in regard to the particular blessings and miracles they are seeking.

For example, they sow financially, when they are believing for financial breakthrough, because the Bible says first give, then second it will be given to you. (Luke 6:38). Similarly, they confess the word of God for their healing while they are trusting God for their bodies to become well.

So, if you want the prayer of Moses, recorded in Psalm 90, to become real in your life, you will need to be consistent and persistent in active faith, appropriate to the specific blessings and miracles you are trusting God to manifest in your life, according to His Word.

What is one thing you have learned from this teaching?

What is one thing you can do to implement this teaching?

Faith Declaration:

I thank You Lord that You are my God, Who puts Your hands of favour and power on the scales of my life to give me success as I live and work by faith, to turn my loss and pain into gain, my mourning into dancing, my frustration into fulfilment, my sickness into health, my poverty into wealth and my depression into joy. I entrust my life to You afresh and prophesy by faith that today will be a good day for me and my family. I step into Your good plans for my life, family, vocation, ministry and future, in Jesus' Name. Amen. I ask and believe You Lord to reveal Yourself to every member of my family and to let everyone around us see Your good and great hand upon us, for Your own glory's sake. Amen.

12   Psalm 23

The Lord is my Shepherd [to feed, guide, and shield me], I shall not lack.
Psalm 23:1 AMP

This is an intensely personal Psalm. That makes it quite different from the Lord's Prayer, which is written entirely in the plural. By doing that, Jesus was subtly teaching us we should not be selfish in prayer but always include others.

The Bible tells us that we cannot change what is written in Scripture in any way. (refer Galatians 1:9 and 5:7-10; Revelation 22:18-19). However, I like to add a word at the beginning of this first verse in order to clarify that the wonderful promises throughout Psalm 23 are conditional, not automatic. The word is "when". So let me take the risk of adding that word to the start of verse one.

> *When the Lord is my shepherd, I shall not want ...... and (going all the way to the end verse 6) ...... goodness and mercy will follow me all the days of my life.*

Now imagine you are being a good sheep of the Lord. You are following the Lord and goodness and mercy are following you. All four of you are walking around in a line, one behind the other. If Jesus turns left, so do you and so do goodness and mercy. If Jesus turns right, so do you and so do goodness and mercy.

What happens if Jesus turns left and you turn right? Let me assure you that goodness and mercy will turn left, because, really, they follow Him, not you. They only follow you, when you follow Him. If you step out of line with the Lord, your Shepherd, then you won't be in the right position to receive all the benefits, blessings and resources He was leading you to.

Goodness and Mercy and all the benefits of Psalm 23 actually follow Jesus, not you. If you follow Him, they will follow you.

Jesus gives Rest and Peace

> He makes me lie down in [fresh, tender] green pastures; He leads me beside the still and restful waters.
> Psalm 23:2 AMP

The Lord knows how to care for his flock, so they are healthy sheep. He provides all we need to succeed. This is the real meaning of this verse and the verse in the "Our Father" prayer: "Give us this day our daily bread."

If more people in this stressful, hectic Western world we live in, would let Jesus be their Lord and Shepherd, they would experience so much more peace and rest and refreshing times in their lives. Jesus Himself reinforced this promise in Matthew 11:28–30.

Jesus heals within

> He restores my soul; He guides me in the paths of righteousness for His name's sake.
> Psalm 23:3 NAS

This is an outstanding promise. When the Lord is your shepherd, He will repair your inner being. Just as Jesus went back to heaven bearing scars, as did the apostle Paul (according to Galatians 6:17), so do we. In Western

Christianity, our scars tend to be internal rather than physical. This is one reason we used this saying as the motto of our children's ministry. "It is better to build children than repair adults."

> *Even though I walk through the valley of the shadow of death, I fear no evil, for You are with me; Your rod and Your staff, they comfort me.*
> *Psalm 23:4*

This great verse is often read at funerals, because the shadow of a loved one's death has come over his or her family and friends.

It is an example of some of the negative things we have inside that the Lord can heal, things like grief, regret and guilt. I remember doing a funeral for a father who died suddenly in a work accident in another country. His sixteen year old daughter was distraught because the last interaction she had with her dad, before he went away, was a bad one.

On one such occasion, the Lord said to me concerning a Christian who had died and the Christian family he left behind: "I will stand in the gap in the lives of those left behind for the one who has gone to eternity." What a wonderful promise that is.

Valleys are tough on both the way down and the way up. We need the Lord with us, whatever direction we are travelling. We also need other people, just as mountain climbers do. Don't be so super-spiritual that you do not recognise your need for God when He has skin on. The Lord normally works through people, as well as doing things Himself.

When you know the Lord is with you, your faith chokes out your fear. You have a greater peace and confidence no matter what the circumstances of your life are, when you have a well-developed personal love relationship and faith partnership with Jesus.

The shepherd's staff was to lovingly keep the sheep in line and rescue them from any slips they made. The rod was a weapon against the enemies of the flock. How encouraging it is to know that the Lord is always ready to pick us up when we fall down. He is also there with us to not only defend us from any attacks we suffer, but to prevent us from being attacked and to bring restoration to our lives for any losses we incur.

Jesus provides for us, regardless of our difficulties

> *You prepare a feast for me in the presence of my enemies. You honour me by anointing my head with oil. My cup overflows with blessings.*
> *Psalm 23:5 NLT*

How great is our God. The fact that we have enemies arrayed against us cannot prevent the Lord getting His abundant blessings and resources through to us.

So when you are faced, not with Hittites, Amalekites and Canaanites as the ancient Israelites were, but with Bill-ites, Sick-ites, Stress-ites and the like, you have an omnipotent Lord and master Shepherd Who can still provide you with all you need and, according to 2 Corinthians 9: 8, enough to share.

That is talking about external adversities such as an economic downturn or the lack of co-operation of key people in our lives. The second part of this verse refers to internal issues that can hinder us from receiving God's provision.

God wants us to have an overflowing cup. Notice the order recorded here. A Christian's head has to be anointed with oil before, by faith, they move into the abundance of grace that God has for them.

Your mind needs to be renewed with God's oil, meaning by His Spirit and according to His Word, before you will experience and overflowing life.

This is what Israel needed before they defeated their foes in the Promised Land. They had to have a positive mind-set before they went to war.

That's why the Lord removed the reproach from them before they began to possess the land God had given them. (Joshua 5:9).

According to Joshua 5:2-8, the army of Israel was circumcised after they crossed the Jordan. In a brilliant display of the Lord's protection in a time of vulnerability, they were not attacked by their nearby enemy, who knew the Israelites were there, during their time of healing.

You can ask God for that kind of protection too. I have sometimes cried out to the Lord, saying: "Don't let any more negativity or pressure touch my life or family or church right now, because we are at our limits and very vulnerable." God has been faithful to me by never allowing me to be tempted more than I can bear. (1 Corinthians 10:13).

The Lord will protect you in your times of vulnerability. Ask Him to do this for you.

> Then the LORD said to Joshua, "Today I have rolled away the shame of your slavery in Egypt." So that place has been called Gilgal to this day.
>
> Joshua 5:9 NLT

God did a transformation for the Jews when they got circumcised. Their shame was rolled away. Their slave mentality, their poverty spirit and other such negative mental attitudes and emotional baggage was removed from them. Their past could no longer sabotage or limit their future.

This is what renewing your mind does. When your head is anointed with the oil of the Spirit and washed with the water of the Word of God, your soul is healed, your mind is transformed. This makes you ready to believe for and embrace the victories and abundant grace that the Lord has prepared for you. Hallelujah.

Lessons From My Dog

Jesus provides good things for you in life and in Heaven forever

Surely goodness and mercy shall follow me all the days of my life; And I will dwell in the house of the LORD forever.
Psalm 23:6

Here's the beautiful thing about having faith in God: you get to taste and see that the Lord is good on earth and in Heaven forever. There's nothing better than that.

Psalm 27 says something that is so very encouraging. It starts with the Psalmist declaring that he will be "confident", regardless of how many enemies are arrayed against him. He declares that his relationship with God is his highest priority and the key to his victory.

In verse 10 he says that even if his parents forsook him, he believed the Lord would pick him up and take care of him. His faith enables him to be confident of something else: *"I will see the goodness of the Lord in the land of the living."* (verse 13).

My point is this: the final verse of Psalm 23 tells us that, when the Lord is our shepherd, we can expect God's favour, provision, love, protection, mercy and goodness in this life, as well as every infinitely good thing in Heaven forever.

With Jesus, it's not just pie in the sky when you die, it's steak on your plate while you wait. Hallelujah!

With Jesus, it's not just pie in the sky when you die, it's steak on your plate while you wait. Hallelujah!

If there is one simple truth you should gain from Psalm 23, it is like a coin a two-sided one. The first side is that Jesus is the most amazing Shepherd anyone could ever have. He will take care of you and provide for you, no matter what happens in your life, nor who else helps you or lets you down.

The second side is that you need to be a good sheep. Love the Lord. Let Him lead you. Trust Him and turn to Him for the resources you need to survive the worst of times, to be sustained in the ordinary and testing times of life and to succeed in both being who you are meant to be and doing what you are called to do through all the times of your life and ministry.

What is one thing you have learned from this teaching?

What is one thing you can do to implement this teaching?

Faith Declaration:

I thank You Lord for all the wonderful promises of Psalm 23 that You have given to me from the moment of my salvation and submission to Jesus as my Saviour, Shepherd and Lord. I am grateful that You help me get through the valley experiences in my life. I praise You as my Provider and Peace-Giver. I rejoice in You, because my enemies cannot prevent You from resourcing me with anointing oil and an overflowing cup. I am grateful for Your goodness, mercy and loving-kindness following me, as I follow You. I give You praise for making me welcome in Heaven and for preparing a place there for me in Your Father's House. Amen.

13 How to have a Healthy Soul:
More like Jesus and More Joy

Dear friend, I am praying that all is well with you and that your body is as healthy as I know your soul is.
3 John 2 NLT

Beloved, I pray that you may prosper in every way and [that your body] may keep well, even as [I know] your soul keeps well and prospers.
3 John 2 AMP

The actual Greek word used by John can be translated as meaning "to have a prosperous journey", or, in other words "to succeed". This translation pictures a person being successful because they are on the right track.

The word "all" means the believer can prosper in every area of life, including spiritually, in family life and all relationships, in ministry, business or career, in finances, in education and in social activities they enjoy.

The apostle John is praying that his dear friend will be as successful in his finances and career and destiny and relationships and bodily health as he is in his inner health. The inner-world health of his spiritual life and of his soul, his mind-will-and-emotions, are important to his physical and outer-world success.

John must have known nearly 2,000 years ago, what is still observable today. Often, the sickness and poverty of a person's soul (i) prevents them from enjoying God and life; (ii) opens the way for sickness to attack their body; and (iii) hinders them from fulfilling their true potential and destiny in Christ.

I want to point out two things about this simple but powerful prayer. Firstly, although it is John's, the very fact that Holy Spirit included it in his epistle means that the Lord intended for us to benefit from it. John was praying from his heart, but his heart was so in tune with God's that his prayer was the same as what the Lord would have prayed.

Secondly, and this is rather obvious, the prayer is a dangerous one. If your soul is not prospering, this prayer works in the negative as well as the positive. Unhealthiness in our soul creates blockages to our faith and to the helping and healing power of Holy Spirit.

Years ago there was a Christian movie called "The Flywheel." Before the central character comes to the Lord in full discipleship commitment, he sells a car to his pastor for an exorbitant price. Before he leaves the pastor's home with his cash, the pastor prays for him. It went something like this: "Lord bless him, as he has blessed me today." The salesman went home with plenty to think about. Maybe he prayed: "Lord, please don't answer my pastor's prayer." You don't have to be the smartest Christian in town to guess which of those two prayers the Lord would answer. I hope you treat your pastor better than that.

In this and the next chapter I will show you six ways by which you can develop a healthier soul.

Become more like Jesus (Romans 8:29)

We become more like Jesus by growing the fruit of the Spirit. (Galatians 5:22-23a). Obviously, the name of this fruit tells us that Holy Spirit helps us grow in this way. However, He doesn't do it for us. We have to use our faith to make such character transformations as replacing anger with peace and depression with joy.

Here is a beautiful and powerful promise we can believe God for and see worked out progressively in our lives: Whatever is not right within you can be changed by the Lord your Shepherd Who restores your soul. (Psalm 23:3a).

Remember, the fruit of the Spirit is not limited to the nine well-known characteristics listed in Galatians. Other Christ-like fruit we develop as we mature in the things of God include holiness, mercy, empathy, generosity, humility, wisdom, courage and servanthood.

> *The merciful man does good for his own soul, But he who is cruel troubles his own flesh.*
> *Proverbs 11:17 NKJV*

When you keep your eyes on Jesus, not on people or incidents or circumstances, your heart will stay healthy. As you continue to behold Him, you will be changed. (2 Corinthians 3:18).

Make room for Joy in your life

We need to cultivate joy in our lives. We have to intentionalise how to experience more joy and then schedule happy times.

In recent years laughing clubs have multiplied around the world. People have found that as they choose to laugh out loud, in company with others who are simultaneously doing the same, their mind-generated laughing becomes as infectious and gratifying as spontaneous laughter. Their mental choice affects their feelings.

I know some Spirit-filled ministers who have done the same, alone in their home or car, in order to cultivate more joy in their lives. I haven't tried it yet.

> A **cheerful heart is good medicine**, but a crushed spirit dries up the bones
> *Proverbs 17:22*

Lessons From My Dog

This verse tells us that our attitudes and emotions, in other words our inner health, have an impact on our physical health. Improving the condition of our soul **_contributes positively to our receiving Divine healing._**

The margin of the New American Standard Bible says that a joyful heart "literally, 'causes good healing.'" In other words, even the Bible recognises that there is a direct, cause-and-effect process: a merry heart produces good healing. Conversely, a broken or crushed spirit has a negative effect on our health (it "dries up the bones").

The state of our soul can certainly and substantially affect our good health or contribute to our lack of it. Doctors sometimes diagnose illnesses as being psychosomatic in origin. This scientific word comes from the same Greek words that the Bible uses for "soul" (the psyche) and "body" (the soma).

Some doctors refuse to acknowledge a miracle when the evidence of one is clearly and irrefutably presented to them. However, the medical world does agree with the Bible and the prayer of the apostle John on this subject, namely, that the state of our inner being can substantially affect our outward physical health, for good or for bad.

Let me give you two specific examples to consider.

> *Men's hearts failing them for fear....*
> *Luke 21:26 KJV*

Is it possible that this is literally true? I think you could easily find many doctors who would agree that people have heart attacks which are triggered by fear.

Secondly, consider the following Scriptures that seem to indicate there is a relationship between grief and poor eyesight. Could this be literally true? I think it could. Psalm 6:7; Psalm 88:9.

> *My eye has grown dim because of grief, and all my members are [wasted away] like a shadow.*
> *Job 17:7*

Notice the second half of this verse in the book of Job introduces a third example of a psychosomatic link, namely, between grief and depression and weight loss. I believe there is such a link. I also know that, for many people depression is a source of weight gain, as they "comfort-eat". They eat not because they are hungry, but somehow eating gives them an up-lift. Unfortunately, like a lot of self-medicated quick fixes, overeating has serious, negative long-term consequences, including depression.

Jesus made it clear that He wants us to experience His joy. (John 16:24; 17:13)

> *These things I have spoken to you so that My joy may be in you, and that your joy may be made full.*
> *John 15:11 NAS*

Joy is one of the fruit of the Spirit in Galatians 5:22. So, as Christians mature in Christ-likeness, they should have more joy. Jesus does not want believers to go around as if they had been baptised in lemon juice. We will have both serious and sad times in life, but that should not exclude regular doses of joy.

All the fruit of the Spirit have to be grown deliberately. We are not all automatically endowed with qualities such as patience, long-suffering and kindness. Even God's kind of agape-love, which is described in 1 Corinthians 13:4-8a, doesn't just grow naturally. It is something we need to develop.

Joy is the same as those other fruit of the Spirit. It requires deliberate cultivation on our behalf in order to grow.

Schedule some fun things in your life. Learn to relax. Live your life according to your own priorities, not someone else's agenda. I learned a long time ago that I cannot be in two places at once. So, I can say no to certain demands on my life, in order to do something I need or even want to do without feeling guilty about it.

For your own health's sake, regularly do some things that make you happy. It might be spending time with your family or playing sport or going to a movie or doing a hobby. If all else fails, get a puppy!

Lessons From My Dog

It is unhealthy and not at all good for your joy-tank to spend too much time alone, even if you are playing your favourite game on your laptop or X-box. Some solitude is good for us, but loneliness leads to depression.

When you are alone, spend quality time with God. Count your blessings. Give Him thanks for the good things in your life. Dream of better days ahead as you walk by faith into the good plans the Lord has for you. (Jeremiah 29:11).

What is one thing you have learned from this teaching?

_____

What is one thing you can do to implement this teaching?

_____

Faith Declaration:

I thank You Lord for empowering me, by Your Word and Holy Spirit to become more like Jesus. Like John the Baptist, I say let Him increase in me, so people see more of Jesus through me. I declare that I am maturing in Christ and that all the fruit of the Spirit will be seen in my life. I thank You Lord for greater joy in my life today and in my future, in Jesus' Name. Amen.

_____

14

How to have a Healthy Soul:
Train your Mind

Dear friend, I pray that you may enjoy good health and that all may go well with you, even as your soul is getting along well.
3 John 2 NIV

Beloved, I pray that you may prosper in all things and be in health, just as your soul prospers.
3 John 2 NKJV

In the previous chapter, I described two ways you can cultivate a healthy soul, namely, by becoming more like Jesus and by cultivating more joy in your life. In this chapter, I will outline a third way, which is the training of your mind.

Renewing your mind leads you into your destiny.

Don't copy the behaviour and customs of this world, but let God transform you into a new person by changing the way you think. Then you will learn to know God's will for you, which is good and pleasing and perfect.
Romans 12:2 NLT

David knew this pattern and result when, under the inspiration of Holy Spirit, he wrote in Psalm 23 verse 5 that first your head has to be anointed with oil and then second your cup will overflow.

When a person becomes a Christian, their spirit comes alive, but their soul and body do not automatically change one hundred percent to demonstrate that they are now Christians. The renewing of our minds is essential to becoming more like Christ, because no-one automatically thinks, speaks, acts or reacts the way God wants us to. We must all learn how to live Christianly. We do this by changing our thoughts, words and actions to be led by Holy Spirit and in accordance with the Word of God so that we think Biblically, Christianly and positively at all times.

When your mind is renewed, you are changed and you begin to walk in the true will of God for your life. According to Romans 12:2, that Divine Will is good for you, acceptable to you and perfect for you. Therefore, you enjoy your life more and you do better in every sphere of life.

Renewing your mind improves your quality of life

As the Word of God renews our mind it also restores and refreshes our soul, it brings us life and radiant health, it imparts Godly wisdom to us and it lifts us spiritually, by boosting our faith.

> *The law of the LORD is perfect, restoring the soul; the testimony of the LORD is sure, making wise the simple.*
> *Psalm 19:7 NAS*

> *Pay attention, my child, to what I say Listen carefully. [21]Don't lose sight of my words. Let them penetrate deep within your heart, [22]for they bring life and radiant health to anyone who discovers their meaning.*
> *Proverbs 4:20-22 NLT*

Lessons From My Dog

> *So then faith comes by hearing, and hearing by the word of God.*
>
> *Romans 10:17 NKJ*

The fact of life is that we are bombarded by so much negativity on a daily basis. It infiltrates our soul, just as grass and dust attach to our body when we mow the lawn.

Bad things that happen to us affect the way we think. It would be great if negative things only affected us in a small way and positive things in a big way. Sadly, all too often, for too many people, it is the opposite of that.

Bad things seem to hit like a hurricane or a bullet even if they are only small and we remember them for a long time. By contrast, we enjoy the moment, but so quickly and easily forget good things after they occur.

Even small, bad things can hit hard and impact us, and we quickly and easily forget good things.

Renewing your mind is like learning a new language

The New Testament talks about renewing our minds, our attitudes, the way we think, because the Lord knows how big a task it is to overcome the implanted teachings of the world and become a person who thinks Biblically, having the Mind of Christ. It's as hard as learning a new language.

The other reason it's like learning a new language is that renewing your mind requires you to renew your mouth. As you change your mind, you change the way you speak .... and vice versa.

Renewing your mind requires you to renew your mouth. As you change your mind, you change the way you speak .... and vice versa.

I am not very good at distinguishing tones in music. For me to learn a tonal language like Chinese would be a lifelong learning experience that I would have to seriously dedicate myself to mastering.

It takes serious commitment to renew your mind with the Word of God. Ephesians 4:22-24 gives us a 3-step pattern to follow:

Firstly, put off your old self – in the words of 2 Corinthians 10:5 "take captive every thought to make it obedient to Christ".

Secondly, be made new in the attitude of your mind.

Thirdly, put on the new self, which I translate, for the purpose of this teaching, as meaning: put on the new mind. Let your thoughts be made like God's thoughts. Learn to think according to what the Bible says.

The rewards of renewing your mind

The rewards of renewing your mind are well worth it. As your mind and attitudes change for the better, your faith grows, you become a better person, you overcome things like depression, confusion and fear, you enjoy your life more, your health gets better, your communication, relationships and your work performance all improve. In other words you begin to prosper in every area of your life, because the prayer of 3 John 2 is coming true for you.

A simple illustration of this is that even the medical profession acknowledges the healing power of good attitudes. The Bible puts it this way:

> *A merry heart does good like a medicine*
> *Proverbs 17:22 KJV*

I was not blessed by starting life as an optimist. It has taken me literally years of faith and years of absorbing God's Word, to develop a healthy soul and a positive mind-set.

One of the most important attitudes to adopt is that of living and functioning as a child of God under His New Covenant of Grace. I don't have to earn God's love or favour. I don't have to perform in a certain way at a required level to get anything from God. All has been given to me freely by grace, because of what Jesus did for me before, on and after the Cross.

Renewing your mind takes deliberate, consistent effort

There is a reason why people talk about the battlefield of the mind. Firstly, your own worldly-educated, proud, rebellious, sin-loving mind does not want to give up control of your life to the Lord. So you have to conquer and crucify the enemy within.

Let me explain what step one in Ephesians 4:22 really means. You must not simply put off your old ways of thinking as you would a shirt that was dirty after wearing it for a day. You might have every intention of wearing it again another day.

Your stinking thinking has got to be put to death. Some thought patterns are so deeply ingrained they have to be put to death a thousand times, or maybe a thousand times a thousand times. You have to replace the old electro-chemical tracks in your brain with new ones built by the Word of God, with the help of Holy Spirit.

The second reason you will have a battle renewing your mind is because the devil will not cooperate with you as you seek to shut out his influences. They include lies, accusations, temptations, discouragements, depression, oppression, and condemnation. The devil knows that he will lose his control over you once you learn to consistently choose right, holy, positive thoughts and reject wrong, sinful, negative ones. Satan is a master at bombarding people's minds, both Christians and sinners, with negativity. You must resist him.

You have to learn how in Christ to wear the helmet of salvation to protect your thought life and how to lift up the shield of faith against every attack of the evil one and how to use the Word of God as your sword of truth and victory over the devil and his demons.

Through faith and persistence, the Lord will help you, to overcome bad mental habits. You will break free of controlling influences such as fear, anger, poverty, lust, greed, inferiority, inadequacy, depression and pride. You will live a new and better life.

Choose to have a positive mind, not a negative one

Look at the contrast these verses make between a negative mind and a positive one. Which would you choose? Which do you choose? Will you choose the right mind and the good fruit of it every day of your Christian life until it is a reality in your thinking, in your emotions and in your life?

> *All the days of the desponding and afflicted are made evil [by anxious thoughts and foreboding], but he who has a glad heart has a continual feast [regardless of circumstances].*
> *Proverbs 15:15 AMP*

> *Those who live according to the flesh have their minds set on what the flesh desires; but those who live in accordance with the Spirit have their minds set on what the Spirit desires. ⁶ The mind governed by the flesh is death, but the mind governed by the Spirit is life and peace.*
> *Romans 8:5-6*

There are some things we can learn from these verses.

(i) If you have a problem with the negativity of your mind, don't just sit around all day, thinking too much.

(ii) You cannot have a positive life, when you have a negative mind. Right thinking leads to victorious Christian living. Stinking thinking leads to mediocrity, negativity, frustration and failure. However, be aware of this: positive thoughts and positive words do not alone or automatically generate success. For example, you can think and speak positively about your career, but if you never apply for a job, you're not likely to get one.

You cannot have a positive life, when you have a negative mind.

(iii) You have to set your mind on the right things. (Philippians 4:8). Positive thoughts are full of faith, hope, and love. Negative thoughts are full of fear, doubt, anger and unforgiveness.

God will and good people can help you reap the benefits of a renewed mind

Here is some good news for you. If you change the way you think, you will change who you are and what you do with your life.

> *For as (a man) thinks within himself, so he is...*
> *Proverbs 23:7a NAS*

You are not alone in this process. You can and should get the help you need from other Christians whose minds and lives have been transformed. You will also have the Lord's help.

> *God has not given us a spirit of timidity, cowardice ... and ... fear, but ... of power, and of love and of calm and well-balanced mind and discipline and self-control.*
> *2 Timothy 1:7 AMP*

It takes time and effort to retrain our minds, but the rewards are worth waiting and working for. God Himself will be with you to empower you in this positive change and personal growth process.

> *For I am confident of this very thing, that He who began a good work in you will perfect it until the day of Christ Jesus.*
>
> *Philippians 1:6*

What is one thing you have learned from this teaching?

_____

What is one thing you can do to implement this teaching?

_____

Faith Declaration:

I thank You Lord for giving me Your Word to renew my mind. I praise You for the help of Holy Spirit to bring my thoughts captive to the obedience of Christ and into conformity with Your Word and the Mind of Christ. I renounce the patterns of thought that have had negative impact on my life and on others, in Jesus' Name. Amen. I dedicate my mind to You, Lord and command it to focus on good, righteous, positive things and produce good fruit in and through my life, in Jesus' Name. So help me God, Amen.

15 How to have a Healthy Soul:
Tame Your Tongue; Move On; Serve Others

Dear friend, I pray that you are doing well in every way and that you are healthy, just as your soul is healthy.
3 John 2 ISV

In the previous two chapters, I described three ways you can cultivate a healthy soul, namely, by becoming more like Jesus, by cultivating more joy in your life and by training your mind. In this chapter, I will outline the final three of the six ways, which are (i) Tame your tongue; (ii) Forgive others, be healed and move on; and (iii) Serve others.

Tame your Tongue

Your words have power and they can do both harm and good. God wants you to use them for good, but the devil wants you to use them for harm. Believers who build enjoyable relationships and enduring ministries, harness the positive power of their tongue. Effective Christians learn to control their tongues and emotions.

> *The tongue has the power of life and death, ...*
> *Proverbs 18:21a*

> *A fool's mouth is his undoing and his lips are a snare to his soul.*
> *Proverbs 18:7*

> *..you have been trapped by what you said, ensnared by the words of your mouth*
> *Proverbs 6:2*

What we speak is a matter of our choice. God wants us to choose to speak for His glory and the blessing and benefit of people. He wants us to choose to not be a mouthpiece for the devil or this sinful world.

Speak for God's glory. Speak for the blessing and benefit of people, including yourself. Choose to not be a mouthpiece for the devil or this sinful world.

We will reap the consequences of how we choose to use our tongues.

> *From the fruit of his lips a man is filled with good things as surely as the work of his hands rewards him.*
> *Proverbs 12:14*

> *The tongue of the wise brings healing*
> *Proverbs 12:18*

Your tongue can bring healing or do harm to others and to yourself.

> *The tongue also is a fire, a world of evil among the parts of the body. It corrupts the whole person, sets the whole course of his life on fire, and is itself set on fire by hell*
> *James 3:6*

Your words not only affect other people and yourself, they also impact Holy Spirit.

> *Do not let any unwholesome talk come out of your mouths, but only what is helpful for building others up according to their needs, that it may benefit those who listen. And do not grieve the Holy Spirit of God, ... Let there be no filthiness (obscenity, indecency) nor foolish and sinful (silly and corrupt) talk, nor coarse gesturing, which are not fitting or becoming: but instead voice your thankfulness [to God].*
> *Ephesians 4:29,30a NIV and 5:4 AMP.*

Having a negative, complaining and critical tongue will sabotage not only your own potential and destiny, but also that of the other people who are damaged by your negative words. It will also ruin the quality of your life and relationships.

> *Whoever would love life and see good days must keep his tongue from evil and his lips from deceitful speech.*
> *1 Peter 3:10*

Forgive; Be Healed; Move On

I think it was Robert Schuller who first used the rhyming verbs in these two sentences: When somebody has hurt you, don't curse it and make it worse; don't nurse it inside and allow it to fester; and don't rehearse it to others who can't help you, so that you pollute and prejudice them, as well as yourself. Instead, disperse it to God in prayer and He will reverse it and work it for good.

Don't curse it, nurse it or rehearse it. Disperse it to God in prayer and He will reverse it.

After all my years in ministry, I have been hurt so many times, I can't even count the number of my scars. I have felt as if I was stabbed in the back, the heart, the head, the stomach and anywhere and everywhere else that it is possible for another person to cause me pain.

I remember one man who waited for a significant church meeting to start and then produced what he thought was evidence of my unsatisfactory leadership. I felt as if he just walked up to me with a knife, pierced me and twisted it to cause the maximum pain and embarrassment that he could. Time and the way I responded to what he did, proved him wrong. Sadly, he backslid after leaving our church.

Another man told people that it was his ministry to empty our church. Praise God, the Lord changed his heart. When I went to see him about his unacceptable behaviour and conversations with others, he had a literal covenant typed up for us both to sign. The covenant was his commitment to never be negative again concerning me or my ministry or the church I was pastoring. When he was reading a Christian book at work on his lunch break, the author used the very words I had said to him on the phone, just 24 hours earlier. He knew God was speaking to him and thankfully he was obedient to what the Lord had revealed in His Word and by His Spirit.

To have a healthy soul, we need to be merciful not judgemental. (Matthew 7:1-5). We need to forgive others. That is a condition of God forgiving us. (Mark 11:24-25). Through exercising mercy and forgiveness you will keep your heart free of poisonous grudges and heart-hardening resentments.

This means you don't keep thinking about the incident over and over. Don't keep complaining to others about how unfairly you were treated and how hurt you still are. How can you get healed if you keep the pain alive?

Instead, get the help you need and disperse your feelings about the situation and the justice of your case in prayer to the Lord. He has promised in Romans 8:28 to turn the situation around for your good ... provided you love Him and are called according to His purpose; in other words, you are doing what God wants you to do with your life.

I have learned that, according to Luke 6:27-28, when dealing with seriously hurtful issues, I have to bless my critics, my "enemies", before I get healed inside: I mean sincerely bless them, not ask God to hit them with a bolt of lightning or a taste of their own medicine. I must ask God to bless them, just as I would want Him to bless me or my friends. Every time I have done that, I have been fully, deeply and permanently healed inside.

In Hebrews 10:17, quoting Jeremiah 31:34, the Bible tells us that God remembers our sins no more. He doesn't develop amnesia. He simply shuts the door of His memory concerning our sins. We have to discipline ourselves to do the same in regard to both (a) sins we have committed but also confessed to the Lord that are washed away by the Blood of Jesus; and (b) sins, hurts and offences that have been committed by others against us.

Whether the person has deliberately or inadvertently hurt you, you must, like God does, both forgive the person and shut the door on the incident/s.

You need to learn to both forgive and forget, by shutting the doors of your mind and your mouth regarding the negative incident/s and the people involved

Let me quote what the Lord taught me from Jeremiah in the book of Lamentations. This is in my book "You Can Prophesy – Supernatural. Simple. Safe."

> *Because of the Lord's great love we are not consumed, for his compassions never fail.* ²³ *They are new every morning; great is your faithfulness.* ²⁴ *I say to myself, "The Lord is my portion; therefore I will wait for him."*
>
> *Lamentations 3:22-24*

"I had to learn, and am still learning, how to shut the door on the past when faced with difficult situations or negative circumstances. This may include the very recent past. Whether someone hurt you years ago or only yesterday, you must learn how to get over it. You can do this by exercising forgiveness, by getting over yourself, and by stepping into the Lord's new mercy, new grace, new love, new blessing, new hope and new power! God has provided these for you each and every day. This good habit, this good love relationship exchange will bring the Lord's victory, healing, peace and joy into your life."

You will also help yourself get healed when you take steps to move forward in your life. I am not saying that as soon as you have a relationship breakdown, you go and find somebody else. That is a recipe for more disaster.

Firstly, get your relationship with God right. Then use Godly wisdom and the enabling of Holy Spirit to rebuild your life inwardly and outwardly. The Lord will help you go forward in every area of your life, one step and one day at a time. God will restore all you have lost. You will experience a positive future, no matter how unlikely it seems when you are wrapped in pain. The time will come, as you stay the course with God, when the joy of the Lord will be your strength. (Nehemiah 8:10).

Secondly, do the natural things you can do to stabilise your emotions and the other areas of your life. I haven't got time in this chapter or book to go into the details of the five stages of grief made famous by Dr. Elizabeth Kubler-Ross, in her best-selling book *On Death and Dying (1969)*, which pioneered people's understanding of this process. Although it was focussed on physical death, the five stages of grief are also experienced to some degree in other areas of life such as in a relationship breakup or through the loss of a job. The stages are: Denial; Anger; Bargaining; Depression; Acceptance.

You have to allow yourself time to go through the process of healing that is appropriate for you. It may take more time and be a different path of recovery than others. That doesn't matter. What does matter is that you get the help and take the time you need to get healthy inside. If your normal eating and sleeping patterns are disturbed, make sure you consult your doctor.

Serve Others

When I was born again and began to go to church regularly, my first pastor had a saying: "We are saved to serve."

In John chapter 15, Jesus taught us that it was in our new Christian DNA to bear fruit, which is the teaching of Paul in Ephesians 2:10.

> *This is to my Father's glory, that you bear much fruit, showing yourselves to be My disciples.*
> *John 15:8*

> *For we are God's handiwork, created in Christ Jesus to do good works, which God prepared in advance for us to do.*
> *Ephesians 2:10*

Some time ago I learned of a testimony told by Matthew Barnett, founder of the Dream Centre in Los Angeles. He said that a lady came to him for counselling for her depression. He spent some time with her and ended by saying he would not make a second appointment until she had spent a week serving in one of their community-oriented ministries. She never returned for further counselling, because she found a satisfying purpose for her life. She was both healed and uplifted by making a positive difference in other people's lives.

Serving others forces you to change your focus from yourself and your needs to God and His answers and to other people and the joy you can bring into their lives.

The fruit for God we are to bear is at least three-fold

(i) The fruit of character, of Godliness, of Christ-likeness, in other words the fruit of the Spirit. (Galatians 5:22-23);

(ii) The fruit of service or good works that are either or both practical and spiritual. (Matthew 5:16; Hebrews 13:16; John 14:12).

In order to bear the fruit of service, it is helpful to discover your own spiritual gifts and the other talents that God has given you which equip you to help and bless others. Rick Warren was the first to describe this process by means of a life and personality matrix he developed which he entitled using the acronym S.H.A.P.E. I added a "D" to the end of his acronym, as you can see from the following words. The matrix enables you to discern your destiny by examining your Spiritual gifts, Heart (passion; motivation), Abilities, Personality, Experiences and Dreams.

(iii) The fruit of spiritual reproduction, that is, winning people to Christ and helping them grow in the Lord. Jesus called this discipleship. (Matthew 28:19; 2 Timothy 2:2).

Conclusion from the prayer in 3 John 2

Your finances and your health matter to God; but the most important thing in your life is the health of your soul and the prosperity of your spiritual life. When you get your inner self healthy, the other areas of your life will improve.

What is one thing you have learned from this teaching?

What is one thing you can do to implement this teaching?

Faith Declaration:

I thank You Lord because where I am weak, You in me are strong. I dedicate my whole being, especially my mind and mouth, afresh to you today for righteousness sake, in Jesus' Name. Amen. I declare that with the help of Holy Spirit my words will edify others and glorify God. I forgive each and all who have hurt or offended me or my family, whether deliberately or innocently. I proclaim Your blessing over them and thank You for my healing. I declare that Your power is in me and Your grace upon me to do good to people in my life today, by natural and supernatural means, in Jesus' Name. Amen.

16 Essential Christian Qualities:
Love and Holiness

And so faith, hope, love abide [faith — conviction and belief respecting man's relation to God and divine things; hope — joyful and confident expectation of eternal salvation; love — true affection for God and man, growing out of God's love for and in us], these three; but the greatest of these is love.
1 Corinthians 13:13 AMP

But you, man of God, flee from all this, and pursue righteousness, godliness, faith, love, endurance and gentleness.
1 Timothy 6:11

There are five essential qualities every Christian must consistently display if they are to fulfil their true potential and destiny in Christ. The five qualities are Faith, Hope, Love, Wisdom and Righteousness.

All of them are necessary, just as we need our head, our arms, our torso, our legs and our feet to be a complete person. Nevertheless, I am going to say something about each of the five in a particular order.

Love is pre-eminent, because God is Love

Love is given pre-eminence in 1 Corinthians 13:13, where the verse says it is the greatest of the three qualities mentioned, faith, hope and love. The primary reason love is pre-eminent is because the Bible says that "God is love." (1 John 4:8) It's not that God has love, He is love.

Essential Christian Qualities: Love and Holiness

When you live by love, you live by the best of all values. You stick to what you believe and how the Bible says you should live, no matter what the devil, people and life throw at you.

When you live by love, you live by the best of all values and you stick with your values, no matter what.

(a) One method of living by love is by implementing the Golden Rule consistently in your decision making and lifestyle.

Do unto others, as you would have them do unto you
Luke 6:31

I have made literally thousands of small and big decisions in my life based on the Golden Rule. It may have been as simple as doing grandma's taxi run with the grandchildren, when my wife was too tired to keep her promise.

Sometimes it was a bigger issue, such as when our church had needs for our building fund at a time when we didn't have much finance. Another fairly local church also needed some building money. So, our church gave up a week's offerings to donate to them. This was not only a love principle, but a faith one, because we believed that as we sowed, so would we reap. God was faithful to us and so were the people who served the Lord with us. When I handed our church over to the next Senior Pastor, we had a debt free property and facilities worth close to three million dollars.

I have to add here that the Lord has a sneaky sense of humour. I say humour because the day we received our give-away offerings, they were bigger than we had received for a long time. I say sneaky because, God was checking whether we were people of our word. Would we give it all away, or would we keep some to meet our own needs. We passed that test and gave it all, unlike Ananias and Sapphira in Acts chapter 5. Sadly, it is also unlike some pastors I have heard of who take up an offering for a visiting minister but only give him a part of what is received.

(b) Another way of living the love life is by blessing people around you. Be an encourager of others, even if you feel as if you need some encouragement yourself. It is an amazing thing that happens time and time again: as you bless and encourage others, strength and joy flow back in to you.

Righteousness ranks second

My second-ranked quality is righteousness, otherwise known as holiness, integrity, morality, ethics and purity.

I rank this second for three reasons:

(a) The Name of God's Holy Spirit.

God Himself chose the Name of the Third Person of the Trinity. He could have called Him Loving Spirit, or Grace Spirit, or Omnipotent Spirit or many other such titles. However, the quality of Holiness was so important to the Lord, that He included it in His Spirit's Name. This quality of the Divine character is so important in Heaven that angels repeat it over and over again: "Holy, Holy, Holy is the Lord God Almighty."

(b) God's love and holiness met at the cross.

God's love forced Him to find a way to exercise judgement over our sin and reclaim the authority over planet earth that Adam and Eve had surrendered to Satan, without hurting us.

God did not want to lose the relationship and partnership He created us to enjoy together. He did not want us to eternally forfeit our friendship with Him, nor our rights as His children to share in His inheritance and to partner with Him in His eternal, as well as His earthly, purposes.

So, Father God sent His Son Jesus to live a perfect life, to be punished for us and to triumph over Satan, sin, sickness and every negative and evil thing on our behalf.

I cannot help shouting Hallelujah right now and I urge you to do the same. How amazing it is, yes it is indeed amazing grace, to realise that Jesus came to get what we deserved, which was punishment for our sins, so that we could get what He deserves which is blessing forevermore.

(c) The seriousness of verses such as Hebrews 6:4-6; 10:26-31; 12:14.

> *This is how we know who the children of God are and who the children of the devil are: Anyone who does not do what is right is not a child of God.*
> *1 John 3:10*

John learned this from what Jesus said in Matthew 7:16-20: *"by their fruit you shall know them."*

It is not enough to know you are clothed with the righteousness of Christ. A true Christian lives righteously, in the practical realities of their daily lives.

> *Therefore, since we have these promises, dear friends, let us purify ourselves from everything that contaminates body and spirit, perfecting holiness out of reverence for God.*
> *2 Corinthians 7:1*

It is not possible to mix darkness with light. You must not live for God on Sunday and the devil the other days of the week. You cannot fool God by putting on a good, religious show in public and in church but live an ungodly, worldly, selfish life when you are out of the Christian spotlight. (Galatians 5:17-21; Hebrews 4:13).

Jesus saved His worst pronouncements for the hypocritical religious leaders of His day. There is nothing that stinks more to God than sin boiled together with religion.

Lessons From My Dog

To live with righteousness means living in integrity, in every area of your life. Be honest, be trustworthy. Be the same in private and in the dark as you are in church and in public. Be of good reputation. Don't cheat on your wife or in your exams.

To live with righteousness means living in integrity, in every area of your life

---

If you live a good and godly life, you won't have to worry about what people say behind your back, because you won't be giving them any ammunition.

That is not to suggest we will never be criticised. Criticism is inevitable and unavoidable. If people criticised the perfect life that Jesus lived, then other negative-minded people will criticise you today. Keep reminding yourself that they have the problem, not you.

Be like the dog on the hunt, who doesn't stop to worry about his fleas. Keep pursuing the purpose of God for your life, which includes becoming more like Jesus and learning how to let Holy Spirit empower you to live a life that pleases God and blesses others.

What is one thing you have learned from this teaching?

What is one thing you can do to implement this teaching?

Faith Declaration:

I thank You Lord that You love me so fully and faithfully and because You fill me with Your love, by Your Spirit. I know I could never earn or deserve Your love and You do not want or expect this. You have given me Your love so freely because of Your Son and Your grace. In Jesus' Name, I declare that by faith and with the help of Your Spirit I will live a life that demonstrates Your love to others. Lord, I am grateful that You consider me righteous in Christ and have clothed me in His righteousness. In Jesus' Name, I declare that by faith and by the power of Your Spirit I will live so that people see the fruit of Christian values and integrity in my life. Amen.

17 Essential Christian Qualities:
Faith, Wisdom and Hope

But now faith, hope, love, abide these three; but the greatest of these is love.

1 Corinthians 13:13 NAS

In the previous chapter, I outlined the first two of the qualities Christians need to live a life that glorifies God and fulfils both their Divine potential and purpose. The qualities of love and holiness are part of the very character and essence of Who God is. Therefore they are essential to be manifested in the lives of people who are made in His image, as we are. The other three qualities outlined in this chapter are: Faith, Wisdom and Hope.

The third of the five essential qualities of Christian living is Faith.

And without faith it is impossible to please God, because anyone who comes to Him must believe that He exists and that He rewards those who earnestly seek Him.

Hebrews 11:6

When we have faith in God and His Word and we use our faith, we will be rewarded by the Lord in this life and in the next.

Essential Christian Qualities: Faith, Wisdom and Hope

All the promises of God are given to us to experience by grace through faith. With faith all things become possible, because there is nothing and no-one that is impossible to the Lord. Our faith empowers us to be His partners and activates His Senior Partnership in our lives.

The thing about faith is that it sometimes requires us to act beyond the understanding of our merely-human minds and to act by overruling our feelings; but we must always act in accordance with the principles of God's Word.

Living by faith means living according to God's Word. From time to time, this will require you to overrule your feelings and not rely on your merely-human understanding.

A great benefit of living by faith is that when you do what the Bible says, God does what the Bible says. For example, if you step out in faith and lay hands on the sick, God will start healing people through you. That is a great reward of faith.

One of the areas of life where too many Christians have difficulty putting their faith into action is in money management. The Lord has given us many promises regarding His rewarding those who handle their finances His way. Let me state it simply: to live by faith with your money, be a giver, not a taker. If you are going to be a taker at all, be a risk-taker for the glory of God.

By faith, be a giver, not a taker. If you are going to be a taker at all, be a risk-taker for the glory of God.

Every Christian should be committed to strengthening their faith in the specific areas in which they are weak. For example, if you are not sure the Lord is your provider, the only way to prove Him (and in Malachi 3:10 the

Lord gives us His specific permission to do this, in this one area of believing His Word), is to adopt His financial principles on a consistent basis. He will demonstrate His faithfulness to you and to His Word. My wife and I have given the Lord the first 10% of our gross income as a tithe plus other giving for more than thirty years. He has never let us down and He never will. He has provided for all our needs and many desires and for all the ministry purposes He has given us to undertake with Him and for His glory.

The fourth essential quality in a Christian's life is Wisdom.

The beginning of Wisdom is: get Wisdom (skillful and godly Wisdom)! [For skillful and godly Wisdom is the principal thing.] And with all you have gotten, get understanding (discernment, comprehension, and interpretation).
Proverbs 4:7 AMP

The fool says in his heart there is no God.
Psalm 14:1

Hebrews 11:6 says we must believe that God exists. It is not enough to believe that some kind of God exists somewhere in the universe. We must believe that the God of the Bible exists and that He is as the Bible describes Him and that He acts in accordance with His Word. That is the kind of Faith which God rewards.

Recently, I had the opportunity to witness to the man who finished off the internal painting my wife Lynne had been doing over recent months. God touched him powerfully, causing his pain to subside and the strength in his elbow and forearm and wrist to increase. He felt the electric heat of the Holy Spirit touch him twice on two consecutive days, for which I praise God.

He said to me: "I have been doing a lot of thinking, but I just don't have the faith that you have." He added: "I believe in the universe." So, I talked to him about God being the only Un-caused Cause in the universe. I told him that it takes much more faith than I have to believe that banging a few rocks together, even for millions of years, could ever create anything that has life, such as a human being or a fish, a flower or a bird.

Living with divine wisdom means living by godly, Biblical principles. To do that, you cannot allow the world to be your teacher, nor let non-Christians shape the way you live.

Let me remind you that wisdom is the brother and co-worker of faith, not its enemy.

Wisdom is the brother and co-worker of faith, not its enemy.

However, some people try to use wisdom as an excuse for unbelief! For example, if God told them to go to China to preach the gospel, they might say: "It's not wise for me to go. It's not the right time for my family, or that country is cracking down against Christians and my presence there would cause difficulties for the local believers." This is not how faith and wisdom interact.

Provided you have done your homework regarding knowing the Will of God, you go by faith. By this I mean that you have sought the Lord regarding His Will and you have checked with godly leaders about what you have been sensing is the Lord's Will. You don't go to China just because one person prophesied it; nor because when you were reading the newspaper (remember them?), it happened to open at a page where China Airlines was offering discounted flights.

Having properly and correctly discerned the Lord's Will, you don't tell the Lord it's not wise for you to go. Rather you ask for His Godly wisdom as to how and when you can go. He will show you how you can obey Him and do it by faith. This is how faith and godly wisdom work together.

Lessons From My Dog

The fifth essential quality of Christian living is Hope.

The rubber hits the road with this quality when a loved one dies. The Bible has an answer with comfort for that.

> ... *we want you to know what will happen to the believers who have died so you will not grieve like people who have no hope.*
> *1 Thessalonians 4:13 NLT*

Biblical Hope is not wishy washy, daydreaming about things that are never going to happen. Biblical Hope is a confident expectation that something God has promised will surely come into the reality of your world even though it hasn't happened yet.

> *Hope that is seen is not hope at all. Who hopes for what they already have?* [25] *But if we look forward to something we don't yet have, we must wait patiently and confidently.*
> *Romans 8:24b (NIV)-25 (NLT)*

What Hope is

Hope is Future-oriented; Faith is Now.

Hope is God saying to Joshua: "Wherever your foot treads, I have given it to you."

Faith is Joshua stepping into the Promised Land and doing battle for what belonged to him, by Divine promise and authority.

Hope can be defined as something God has promised us that motivates us to act in ways which bring the things we are hoping for into reality in our lives. I believe that Hope inspires Faith. Faith grows in the garden of Hope.

If you can hope for something, if you can visualise it happening, you can begin to believe that it will happen. If you see it in God's word; if you can imagine that what God promises can become a reality in your life, then your faith will grow until it is strong enough to claim your Biblical inheritance.

The second meaning of Biblical hope is the vision or purpose to which God has called you. This definition of hope reminds and motivates us to get into alignment with our divine assignment. Put the purposes of God at the top of your to-do list, not at the bottom.

Hope is the soil in which faith grows. Hope motivates us to live according to God's promises and purposes

To live with hope is to be motivated to bring the promises and purposes of God into reality in and through your life and ministry. To live with hope is to live according to a God-given vision of His Divine purposes for your life.

Conclusion re 5 essential Christian Qualities

If a believer cultivates and operates in life according to these five Christian qualities, he will radiate the fragrance of Jesus. He will be effective in the Kingdom of God. He will live an exemplary and enjoyable and fruitful life that glorifies God and benefits people in his sphere of influence.

I encourage you to not allow the devil, people or any kind of circumstance, pressure, hurt or offence to cause you to waver from living your life according to these five essential Christian qualities: Love, Righteousness, Faith, Wisdom and Hope.

What is one thing you have learned from this teaching?

What is one thing you can do to implement this teaching?

Faith Declaration:

I thank You Lord for giving me the measure of faith I need to succeed in fulfilling my divine potential and destiny. Thank You for helping me grow in faith until all things become possible to me as they are to You. I thank you that my faith is sufficient for any and every situation I face, whether positive or negative, whether an opportunity or a challenge. I am grateful for Your wisdom. I declare that I have the mind of Christ and that as a son of God, I am led by Your Spirit. I praise You for giving me good, godly, wise people as counsellors, who help me make good decisions and keep me accountable to live by Your principles. I declare that I have confident expectation of Your promises coming to pass in my life. I decree that the purposes of God for my life will surely come to pass, in Jesus' Name. Amen.

18   24 hour Prayer
to Save a Multitude

Rescue others by snatching them from the flames of judgment.
Jude 1:23a NLT

Jesus answered him, "Truly I tell you, today you will be with Me in paradise."
Luke 23:43

According to current statistics, around 150,000 people die each day. That's nearly two people every second or every never-ending handclap. Whether young or old, rich or poor, male or female, educated or uneducated, overweight or underweight or in as good condition as a professional athlete, more than 100 human beings around the world will face their Maker every minute. That's over 6,000 per hour and more than 55 million per year. We Christians need to be praying for them to get saved before they meet the Lord face-to-face.

Just a few years ago in Victoria, a young 14-year old girl was picked up for a ride by a group of teenagers. She soon realised the driver was far too drunk to drive responsibly. They stopped at McDonalds to get some fast food. Unfortunately, she was not emotionally strong enough to refuse to get back in the car and then call her mum to come and pick her up. The group all piled back into the car. The drunk took the wheel and sped off. After a short time, the young girl sent her last text to a friend: "I'm afraid I am going to die." Sadly, a few minutes later, she did.

The two Scriptures at the beginning of this chapter tell us two things. Firstly, when the Lord answers this prayer, He spiritually snatches souls out of the very doors of Hell, out of the sulphurous snares of the devil. Secondly, when Jesus saved a thief on a cross near the end of his last day on earth, He gave us a Divine example of His willingness to save even criminals in their last hours.

A friend of mine came over from Western Australia to receive prayer at a large healing meeting in Brisbane. The night I took him there, thousands of people attended. They filled the huge auditorium. My friend got a touch from the Lord, but not a complete healing.

While I was praying for him that night, I began to intercede for everyone present who needed a healing. Holy Spirit said to me: "Why confine yourself to the walls of the building?"

That's when I began to pray lots of global prayers. I pray for souls and for revival in every nation. Based on the part of Lord's Prayer that says "Give us this day our daily bread", I also pray for the Lord to do many food and water miracles around the world. I ask Him to multiply food, to make dirty water clean and to provide streams in the desert. I call down rain as Elijah did. I pray that God will do these miracles in ways that bring Him glory, as well as meet human needs.

The greatest prayer the Lord showed me was based on the word "daily" in that same line of the Lord's Prayer. Holy Spirit led me to pray and ask as many Christians as I could influence to join me in this same prayer. That's why this chapter is included in my book.

The prayer is that people will hear the Gospel and respond to Christ in the last 24 hours of their life on earth. That includes the last 24 nano-seconds of their life.

Please pray with me that many people will be saved in the last 24 hours of their life on earth.

This could happen by any of three means: (a) a person, whether family, friend or stranger; (b) Christian media, such as a Bible, television, radio, a tract, a book, a CD, a DVD or an online teaching. This revelation is what inspired me to believe in the Kingdom power of the internet and Facebook and Christian television and radio; (c) a supernatural intervention of the Lord Himself, a Holy Spirit inspired vision or dream or the visit of an angel.

On one occasion Holy Spirit gave me this amazing glimpse into the day I walked into Heaven: An angel met me. He was going to take me to the Throne Room to meet my Heavenly Father, my Lord and Saviour, Jesus and my Helper, Holy Spirit. As I looked over to my right, I saw a massive crowd of people. They were just milling around until I turned to look at them. Suddenly they burst into exuberant praise to God and His Christ. They lifted up holy hands and praised with all their might. I asked the angel: "Who are they?" He replied: "They are the ones who were saved in answer to the prayer the Lord gave you to pray and to share with others."

So, when I heard the sad news report concerning the young girl to whom I referred above, I had the satisfaction of knowing that I had prayed for her salvation. I hope she is one of the crowd I saw praising the Lord in heaven.

I invite you to share in interceding for people like her by praying for people to be saved in their last 24 hours on earth.

I will add that I have subsequently extended my prayer to include people receiving Gospel revelation in their last 24 days and 24 weeks.

I extended the time-focus of my prayer because of the testimony of my dad. In the last months of his life, he loved me reading the Bible to him, especially the Parable of the Sower. However, for some reason, dad refused to give His life to Jesus, by praying the sinner's prayer. I couldn't understand why he was so enthusiastic for the Word, yet so reluctant to get saved.

I took my pastor along. He asked dad what was the reason for his reluctance. Because he didn't understand the Grace of God, dad said something like: "I am not worthy to be saved. I have made mistakes. I have sinned. I don't think I should cheat the system by getting saved so late in life."

My pastor shared the testimony of the thief on the cross next to Jesus. Dad was so impacted by that. He gave his heart to the Lord. On the night he died, Holy Spirit spoke to me through His Word, from Psalm 61 verse 7 in the King James Version. *"He shall abide before God forever."* I went to sleep in peace.

We sang that Psalm at dad's funeral, which was only a few weeks later.

Please pray with me that many people will be saved in their last 24 hours, 24 days or 24 weeks of life.

I believe in Bible verses that talk about household salvation (Genesis 6:18; Psalm 103:17; Isaiah 54:13; Jeremiah 32:38-41; Joel 2:28; Acts 2:38-39; Acts 16:31). The miracle of the Passover in Exodus chapter 12 is another type of household salvation. The blood of the sacrificed lamb protected the whole family inside the Israelite homes. The Egyptian children were not saved, because there was no blood of the lamb over their houses.

What is one thing you have learned from this teaching?

What is one thing you can do to implement this teaching?

Faith Declaration:

I praise You for sending Jesus to save us and rescue us from all the works of the devil. I thank You Lord because You can save people anywhere, anytime, no matter who they are or how far from You they are. I thank You for the promise of household salvation. I declare in Jesus' Name that my family will come to the Lord and many souls be saved during their last day on earth, in every nation. I speak prosperity to every Gospel-preaching person, church and ministry organisation on earth, in Jesus' Name. Amen.

19 Defeating the Disappointment Spiral

And hope does not disappoint us, because God has poured out His love into our hearts by the Holy Spirit, whom He has given us.
Romans 5:5

In 1858, the Democrat-controlled Illinois legislature sent Stephen Douglas to the US Senate. They had benefitted from a gerrymandered electorate that enabled them to overrule the fact that Abraham Lincoln had won the popular vote. A friend asked Lincoln how he felt. The answer, given by the man who lost virtually every election he contested until he became possibly the greatest President in the history of that great nation, was this: "Like the boy who stubbed his toe, I am too big to cry and too badly hurt to laugh." (Source unknown).

Disappointment is something that affects every person on the planet. Some handle it better than others. If someone does not treat the disappointment in a correct and timely manner, it can become like a small injury that gets infected. The infected area will get worse still and eventually become a serious health issue if remedial action is not taken.

If you will pardon me being a little graphic in my description, I have told many people that it is better to deal with problems at the pimple stage, not the cancer stage.

Defeating the Disappointment Spiral

Deal with problems at the pimple stage, not the cancer stage

The Disappointment Spiral shows how negative attitudes that are not attended to get worse, not better:

(1) Disappointment

(2) Discouragement

(3) Disillusionment

(4) Distorted perspective

(5) Depression

(6) Distance

(7) Distrust

(8) Disbelief

(9) Deception

(10) Disobedience

(11) Despair

(12) Defeat

(13) Death, perhaps of a marriage, a career, a ministry or a dream. Sadly, in some instances, the disappointment spiral has ended in suicide.

Here are a few brief observations about each of these 13 steps in the Downward Spiral.

(i) Dis-appointment can be like a poison that slowly infects your whole system and lifestyle. I like the saying: "By grace through faith, we can turn disappointments into His-appointments."

(ii) Dis-couragement weakens a person, because he cannot overcome life's pressures and challenges without courage.

(iii) Dis-illusionment robs him of hope and vision. He starts to become double-minded. This opens the door to confusion.

(iv) Distorted perspective. At this point he begins to get negative, resentful, angry, depressed and tired.

(v) Depression and fatigue get a strong grip on the downward-slider. Some may even succumb to self-medication and chronic fatigue, because "hope deferred makes the heart sick." As his dreams appear to be going into reverse or his problems look like they are getting bigger and more impossible to solve, he starts to sink deeper into the mire.

(vi) Distance. He begins to neglect God and withdraw from people. His world gets smaller. He is more self-focussed. He starts to make himself feel worse. He blames God and other people for his situation. He may step back from relationships, because other people's joy makes his frustration harder to bear. If he has drinking too much or taking drugs, his guilt and shame as well as his depression push him away from God and people in his life.

(vii) Dis-trust of people. He gets suspicious and critical of others.

(viii) Dis-belief of God and His Word. He stops believing that God is good, all the time; and that He is great and faithful and impartial, meaning that the Lord will act for everyone, not just for the select or especially favoured few. At this point, he is defaming God's character and dis-honouring His Word. How can a person believe God is the Answer, when he is treating Him as if He was the cause of the problem?

(ix) Deception. This may start as purely spiritual in nature, such that the person believes the lies of the devil about God and His Word. It escalates to being deceived by the world, by his own negative inner sinful nature and by the devil about many different things including God, people, himself, the reality of his actual situation, alternative solutions and potential outcomes.

(x) Disobedience. When the person becomes disobedient, he feels worse, not better. At this point he can really hurt himself or others or lead them astray. He gets rebellious and angry, which causes him to do things to "cut off his nose to spite his face." Internal guilt and shame build up inside even though he buries all these negative feelings deep inside and pretends they are not there.

(xi) Despair. He feels like a failure. He thinks he is useless and his situation is hopeless. He believes that God doesn't care and won't help him.

(xii) Defeat. Winston Churchill first said what is quoted by many sports people and motivational speakers: "Success is not final, failure is not fatal: it is the courage to continue that counts."

(xiii) Death. This might be of a marriage, career, ministry, dream or even literal suicide, which is absolutely devastating for those whom are left behind. Our God specialises in the resurrection of broken hearts and dreams. He can restore you with double portion blessing as He did in the last chapter of the Book of Job. Don't you just love a happy ending!?

Did you notice how many words beginning with "dis" are in that downward spiral?

One of the dictionary definitions of "dis", taken from Roman mythology, is the ruler of the underworld. This is a reminder that Satan is either the source or the exaggerator of all the "dis" we suffer from. We must resist him in the Name of Jesus, so that he does not rob us of our blessings and inheritances as the children of God.

Our enemies are not Philistines, like Israel fought in the Old Testament. The New Testament tells us that our enemies are not "flesh and blood" individuals. Our enemies do include negative attitudes, thoughts and emotions in our mind and, as Ephesians 6:12 says, "rulers ... authorities ... powers of this dark world and ... spiritual forces of evil in the heavenly realms."

These enemies cause us to slip down the Disappointment Spiral. They have lots of names, such as dis-ease, dis-unity, dis-comfort, dis-grace, dis-tress, dis-may, dis-respect, dis-aster, as well as all thirteen problems listed in the Spiral itself, and many other things that put downward pressure on our lives.

There is a story told that the devil was having a garage sale. He was in Australia at the time. If he was in USA, he would have had a yard sale. Remember, he can only be in one place at a time. The Lord is everywhere, with you, all the time.

As he put prices on all his weapons, the new demons noticed that two of them, like a knife and fork set, were priced far more expensively than the others like anger, lust, greed, fear, guilt and shame. They were very curious about why he valued these two old and worn weapons so highly.

Satan said: "Because when I use disappointment and discouragement, they open the door of the person's life to all the other weapons I have."

The enemy has a strategy to get a foothold in your life and progressively turn it into a stronghold. Your job is to resist him and with the Lord's help escape his clutches and exercise your God-given authority in Christ to enforce Jesus' victory over him.

I want to tell you that our God specialises in releasing uplifting power. He is the wind beneath our wings. (Isaiah 40:31).

Our God specialises in releasing uplifting power. He is the wind beneath our wings.

He can lift us from the bottom to the top and way over that. Remember, Jesus Himself acknowledged that there is a devil who tries his hardest to ruin our lives; but Jesus also said: "I have come that they might have life more abundantly, life to the full, life till it overflows, rich and satisfying life." (John 10:10 various versions).

The Lord doesn't lift us up without our faith and participation. When you are on the spiral, you must want to get off it. You must be willing to use your faith to climb back up that spiral, in the same way the prophet Elijah did.

Defeating the Disappointment Spiral

In 1 Kings 19, Elijah suffered an attack of suicidal depression because of the threat on his life by the evil Queen Jezebel. He walked forty days and nights to the cave on Mount Horeb. Elijah met God there. The Lord asked: "What are you doing here, Elijah?" (verse 9). This tells us that Christians do not belong on the Disappointment Spiral.

Then the Lord said to Elijah: "Go back the way you came ...". (verse 15). In other words, we need to put our faith to work with the Lord, and any of His helpers, so that we get off the Disappointment Spiral and get flying with eagles as Isaiah 40:31 tells us we can.

There are both natural and spiritual things we can do to climb back up the Disappointment Spiral, no matter how far down we have slidden.

Alcoholics Anonymous espouse the 12 steps. That's helpful, but only if your higher power is the Triune God, Father, Son and Holy Spirit, because They will help you get healthy, strong and positive. The other necessity for these 12 steps to work is that you build your faith and shape your life according to the Word of God. Their idea of having others help you is not just a good one, it's an essential component of walking in victory, freedom and confidence. Those people need to be other Christian believers, who are representing the Lord on earth is another good idea that A.A.

Rick Warren's Saddleback church began what is now an international ministry called "Celebrate Recovery". It is designed to help people overcome the bad effects of hurts, habits and hang-ups they have in their lives. The ministry is based on the Beatitudes of Jesus and is highly recommended because it is Christ-centred and Bible-based. It is also Holy Spirit empowered and not just dependent on the mind- and soul-power and self-help of purely human psychology. The program was begun as a "Christianised" alternative to A.A.'s "higher power" approach.

How to Climb back up and off the Disappointment Spiral

(i)   Change your expectations so that you accept disappointments are part of life and are useful for growing in maturity and strength and for training in love, faith, wisdom and godliness. There is an old saying: "Expect the best, but prepare for the worst."

Prepare yourself spiritually, mentally and emotionally for disappointments and discouragements before they touch your life. When my mum turned 85, I started to prepare myself for her departure into eternity to be with the Lord, by saying to myself, mum's only got a few years to go. It helped me be ready for when that day came. I praise God that all four of my and my wife Lynne's parents are in Heaven.

(ii) Trust in the nature and power and sovereignty of God, no matter what happens or doesn't happen. When David lost everything at Ziklag, the Bible says he strengthened himself in the Lord. You can and should do that too. Get closer to God every day of your Christian life. Don't allow disappointment to drive you from God. Letting that happen just gives the devil opportunity to weaken your faith and rob you of your Divine Relationship, Partnership and Inheritance that is yours in Christ. Instead, resist the devil and he will surely flee from you. It may not be in round 1 of your fight, but you will win the good fight of faith, because Jesus has already won the victory for you. So, the devil will surely flee from you at some point, if you keep pressing into God and pressing on in Him.

(iii) Start to climb up the very same set of stairs you went down. There is a great story told of a donkey who fell into a disused well. The farmer couldn't be bothered rescuing the animal which was past his prime. He decided to fill in the well. Every time the farmer threw in a pile of dirt or rubbish, the stubborn mule stood up, shook himself off and stepped up on to the next layer of material that would one day enable him to step out of that well. Sure enough, the day came when the donkey did just that. We have to learn how to shrug off the bad stuff that touches us and keep going onward, forward and upward, no matter how slow or difficult our progress may be. Keep shaking off life's downers and dirt and set-backs and for sure, one day, you will step up and out of your unfair, negative situation.

(iv) Take responsibility for yourself, your feelings, your words and your behaviour. What is responsibility? It is the ability to choose your response. Change your mind-set from negative to positive, any way and every way you can. Casting your cares on the Lord, because you know He cares for you, is one way to do this.

Rejoice in the Lord always and again I say rejoice
Philippians 4:4

If you read this epistle of Paul's closely, you will discover that is it an epistle of making choices. We must choose (and keep on choosing) to overcome disappointment. There comes a time for all the negatives in our lives, big and small, many and few, when we need to get over it and get on with it. This is not a quick or easy thing to do. With the Lord's help, and by faith, all things are possible.

The choices we must make include the choice to rejoice in the Lord. This is the choice to praise the Lord always and to praise Him anyway, which means regardless of what negativity you are having to deal with in your life. Rejoicing in the Lord also means that you get and keep yourself spiritually healthy, so that His joy can be your strength.

Don't make hasty, big solo decisions, such as quitting your job, when you are on a "downer". Rather, choose to make the decisions you have to make in order to improve your life.

(v) Admit your need to yourself, to God and to others. Then get the help you need to overcome your problems. Don't tell people you "don't care" about something, when in reality you do care about it, because it has hurt you, depressed you or made you angry.

(vi) Forgive others. Put aside all thoughts of taking revenge or wishing them a "taste of their own medicine". Pray for those who hurt you. Let things go and move on with your life. In some nations, some clever hunters discovered a way to catch monkeys. They would put special treats in a tin that the monkeys could reach into. The tin was nailed to a tree. The monkey would clench its fist around the treat only to discover that it could no longer get its hand out of the tin. If it stubbornly clung on to the treat, it remained captive until the hunter returned to capture it. If only the monkey had let go of the bait, he could have gone free. Refusing to let go of negativity, keeps a person in captivity.

(vii) Be both persistent and patient. (Hebrews 6:10-12; Hebrews 10:35,36). Keep praying and keep doing what you know is right to do. Your harvest, your reward, your healing and your provision will surely come in their due season. I remember being powerfully impacted by this saying: "Things work out best for those who make the best out of how things work out."

(viii) Cultivate contentment in all circumstances of life, as Paul did. (Philippians 4:11b-13). Contentment is not the fulfillment of what you want to have. It is the appreciation of what you do have.

(ix) Deliberately schedule wise and legal fun times in your life.

(x) Deliberately build positive friendships in your life.

(xi) Start every new day with fresh faith, believing as Jeremiah did that God's mercies are new every morning and His steadfast love for you never ceases.(Lamentations 3:22-23). You must live your best life in the now, not dwelling on the past, nor wishing it was already the future, because those two options lead only to depression. Of course we know that God is Lord of the past, the present and the future; but the Name He gave Himself was "I AM". This Name means that God is saying He has covenanted to be with you in the now of your life both to be and to do whatever you need the "I AM" to be and do. As you, in relationship and covenant partnership with God, make the best of your "now", your future will become all that the Lord has prepared for you.

(xii) Keep your eyes on Jesus, on things unseen. (2 Corinthians 4:16-18; Hebrews 12:1-2). When you trust God and put your faith and hope in Him you will not be disappointed, because He is a covenant-keeping, miracle-working God, Who is Good & Who has a good plan for your life. As you focus on Him and His Word, you will begin to hope for and believe for better days. This faith lift will help you climb back up, even run back up, even fly back up that up that Disappointment Spiral and soar with God into a great future.

Defeating the Disappointment Spiral

Shout for joy, O heavens; rejoice, O earth; burst into song, O mountains! For the LORD comforts his people and will have compassion on his afflicted ones. [14] But Zion said, "The LORD has forsaken me, the Lord has forgotten me." [15] "Can a mother forget the baby at her breast and have no compassion on the child she has borne? Though she may forget, I will not forget you! [16] See, I have engraved you on the palms of my hands; your walls are ever before me. [22a] This is what the Sovereign LORD says: [23b] those who hope in Me will not be disappointed."

Isaiah 49:13-16,22-23

What is one thing you have learned from this teaching?

What is one thing you can do to implement this teaching?

Faith Declaration

I thank You Lord that You are truly the wind beneath my wings. You are my glory and the lifter of my head. You are the One Who enables me to walk with my head held high. I thank You that I can and will, by faith, step into the abundant life Jesus purchased for me. I renounce every work of the devil that has affected my life, in Jesus' Name. I resist every negative force, thought and emotion that has been pushing me onto the Disappointment Spiral. I forgive every person who has impacted my life for worse, not better. I put my faith into action to rise higher than I ever have before. Amen.

20 Praising our Covenant-Keeping Lord

When God introduced Himself to Moses at the burning bush, He called Himself "I AM". This tells us several things about the Lord.

Firstly, He is God, the only self-existent, eternal being. He is the Uncaused Cause of the Universe and all in it. He always was, is and forever will be.

Secondly, the Lord is always in the present moment and He is present in the present moment as God.

Thirdly, because God did not qualify His Lordship in any way, it indicates He is Lord in every way. Hallelujah. In other words we can assure the sinner, that God says to them: "I AM your forgiving Saviour." To the sick, He says: "I AM your Healer." To the poor, God says: "I AM your Provider." To the stressed and depressed, the Lord says: "I AM your Peace." In the practicality of your need, in your time of need, God, The Lord is all you need.

God, the Lord, is your wisdom, strength, righteousness and victory. He is your Shepherd, Helper, Teacher, Guide and Empowerer. The Lord your God is all you need to succeed!

Over a period of time, this Name became to be known as Jehovah. At various times The Lord revealed Himself in ways that described His Nature and Divine attributes. His original Name became linked to other descriptive Names. There are eight commonly known redemptive, or covenant, Names of God, Who revealed Himself as I AM, YHWH, Jehovah.

The eight Names are: Jehovah Tsidkenu; Jehovah Mkaddesh; Jehovah Roi; Jehovah Shalom; Jehovah Shammah; Jehovah Rapha; Jehovah Jireh; Jehovah Nissi. Using those Names in prayer and praise is one of my favourite ways to express my love for, adoration to and faith in my Lord. Below are some ideas on how you can do the same.

(i)   Jehovah Tsidkenu

God, I praise You for being the Lord our righteousness. I praise You Father, because You are righteous and You always do what is right. I thank You for giving me the righteousness of God through Jesus my Saviour.

(ii)   Jehovah M'Keddesh

God, I praise You for being the Lord Who sanctifies. I thank You that, when I became born-again in Christ Jesus, You empowered me, by Your Holy Spirit, to live a holy and productive life, which is pleasing unto the Lord and honours God. I thank You, Holy Spirit, because You enable me to overcome the sin, negativity and bad habits in my life and You equip me to serve the Lord by serving people, as a vessel of honour, fit for the Master's use and ready for my God-given destiny.

(iii)   Jehovah Roi

God, I praise You for being the Lord My Shepherd.

I thank You, Father, for making all the promises in the Bible, including those in Psalm 23, belong to me because I have accepted and submitted to Jesus Christ, Your chief Shepherd, as my Lord. Therefore, I thank You that I shall not want, because Goodness and Mercy shall follow me all the days of my life. I am grateful to know that as my good Shepherd, You will always take care of me and make me a healthy, happy and productive member of Your flock.

(iv) Jehovah Shalom

God, I praise You for being the Lord our Peace. I praise You because You bring peace to troubled souls, relationships and situations. I am grateful that You impart Your Peace to me, even in illogical situations, because I choose to put my focus on and trust in You.

I thank You because Your peace affects every area of my life. By faith in the sacrifice and triumph of Jesus, I have peace with God, within myself, in my body, in my relationships and partnerships, in my finances, in my circumstances and in my ministry. I praise You for the peace I have knowing that You are watching over me, protecting me and all that is dear to me.

I thank You Lord for the fact that, when I cast my cares on You, as I do now, in Jesus' Name, You carry them for me and from me, because You care for me. I trust You to take care of me and of everyone and everything that I care about.

I honour You as the God of peace and believe that You will soon crush Satan under my feet. Lord, by faith, I receive Your peace afresh today.

(v) Jehovah Shammah

God, I praise You for being Emmanuel, the Lord Who is always present with me, anywhere, everywhere, all the time. I thank You that You are with me always, as the greatest One, in Whom there is all power and authority in Heaven and on Earth. I thank You Lord, because You are a faithful, Heavenly Father to me. No matter what situation I am in, You are always there for me, You always come through for me and You always work all things together for my ultimate good.

I thank You Lord because You are for me, so who can be against me? It's a source of great comfort and confidence to me to know that You are on my side and by my side. Therefore, I will not fear bad news, nor what man or the devil may attempt to do to me and mine. Lord, I believe that nothing is going to happen to me that You and I together can't handle.

I praise You Lord because Your presence with me empowers me to do Your work and will on earth, which blesses people and glorifies You.

(vi) Jehovah Rapha

God, I praise You for being the Lord our Healer. I thank You Father that You are the Lord Who heals me and Who enables me to live my life in Your health. Thank You Lord, for Your desire that I should prosper and be in health, according to the measure of my prosperity in my spiritual and inner life.

I thank You Jesus for bearing my sicknesses, diseases, pains, afflictions, griefs and sorrows on the Cross. By Your wounds I am healed, both in my inner man and in my physical body. Thank You Lord, for paying the price for my total well-being.

I thank You Holy Spirit for living within my body and for releasing God's healing power within me, according to my needs and my faith. Thank You for giving me Your Word which is life and health to my whole body and Your joy within me which does me good like a medicine.

I thank You Lord for equipping me as a believer in Christ and choosing to use me in the ministry of healing. I praise You because the Bible says that when I lay hands on the sick, believing, in Your Name, then they shall recover. Thank You for giving me Your authority and anointing me with Your Power to heal, for the Glory of God.

(vii) Jehovah Jireh

God I praise You for being the Lord Who will see to it, Whose provision shall be supplied and seen. I thank You Father that You have committed Yourself to supplying all that is needed, both practical and spiritual, for my life, my family, my ministry and my Church, according to Your abundant riches in glory in Christ Jesus. I honour and appreciate You, Lord, as the God of plenty, the One Who is more-than-enough for my every need, desire and opportunity. You are the absolutely reliable and infinitely inexhaustible Source of every good thing in my life.

I bless You because You are so rich, so kind and so generous. I thank You for Your unmerited favour towards me which is evident, because in and through Christ You have granted me all things pertaining to life and godliness, including every spiritual and practical blessing, so that I have an abundance for every good work.

I praise You because You give me the power to make wealth. Therefore, I claim and declare that whatever I put my hand to do shall prosper, as I live in and serve You by faith.

I thank You Lord for allowing me to prove Your faithfulness and generosity by the giving of my freewill offerings and my tithes, which belong to You, to my local Church. I thank You for opening the windows of Heaven over me and mine, and pouring out Your blessing upon us so freely, according to our obedience, love and faith in giving.

I thank You for rebuking the devourer of our finances so that we do not lack for any good thing. I declare in Jesus' Name that there is no recession in the Kingdom of God and that therefore, by faith, we will not live in lack, but in both the sufficiency and abundance of Your supply.

(viii) Jehovah Nissi

God I praise You for being the Lord my Banner. I thank You Lord that Your banner over me proclaims Your love and victory over my life. I praise You, because Your Love for me is constant and unfailing. I am grateful Lord that You loved me first and You love me faithfully. I love you in return.

I praise You Lord God Almighty, because You have limitless power and strength. You are my help, my strength and my shield. You are the Lord, the All-Sufficient One. You make the impossible become possible to anyone and everyone who believes in You and Your Word. There is nothing and no-one that is too hard for You. You are the God of miracles, Who is always ready, willing and able to do exceedingly abundantly more than all that I can ask or think. Lord, You are the greatest of the great and the best of the best forever.

I rejoice in You, because I am born again, born to win, because my battles are Your battles and victory belongs to the Lord. I thank You for equipping me in Christ to be more than a conqueror. I praise You, because Your Holy Spirit always leads me into victory, by giving me the ability, strategy and opportunity to win, against all odds, in every situation, by faith, to the glory of God. Thank You Lord for enabling me to possess my promised land, fulfil my potential and destiny, and lead others into victory, for Your Glory's sake.

I conclude this chapter with a faith challenge for you: Faith is not like a single rock that is either big or large. Faith is like a forest, a group of trees. Some trees can be very young or weak and small. Other trees can be so strong, deep-rooted, solid and so full of life that no storm of wind, rain or fire can stop them from producing fruit and new life.

Your faith is probably strong in terms of some of the Names of the Lord I have shared here, but weak when applied to one or more of the other aspects of the Lord's covenant partnership in your life.

My challenge to you is develop your faith in all areas of God's covenant revelation. Build your faith until you believe equally that God is your Righteousness (you are saved because you have received the righteousness of Christ by faith), your Sanctification (He helps you to live a holy life), your Shepherd, your Peace, your Companion (Who is with you always, everywhere), your Healer, your Provider, your Victory and the Lover of your soul.

What is one thing you have learned from this teaching?

What is one thing you can do to implement this teaching?

Faith Declaration:

I thank You Lord for being the faithful covenant-keeping Lord Who has all power to fulfil Your promises. I praise You because You are not a man who would lie or change Your mind. I exalt You, because You watch over Your Word to perform it. I am so grateful that I am never alone in relationship or partnership because You are always with me in all Your covenant abilities. Amen.

21 The Lord's Banner Over You

Moses built an altar and called it The Lord is my Banner.
Exodus 17:15

Too many people have been "labelled" by negativity spoken over them by other people in their lives.

Some time ago, Holy Spirit gave me a memorable visual impression of what the banner of the Lord means to His New Testament people.

There are two meanings.

The first is the one found in Exodus chapter 17:8-16. It is the account of Joshua's victory over the Amalekites on the battlefield at Rephidim. Whenever Moses held up his hands in prayer, Joshua would win the battle. When Moses' hands drooped down, the Amalekites would surge again and the battle would turn in their favour. What a lesson about the power of prayer.

The rod Moses was holding up was spiritually important. It is referred to in Scripture as the rod of God (Exodus 4:20). In those days it would have had inscribed on it the Name of the Lord, some family names and history, and probably some promises of God or quotes from their history with God. The point is that raising the staff represents lifting up the Name and Word of God in prayer.

When you read the Bible's description of this great victory, you also see the power of partnership in both prayer and action. Aaron and Hur helped the tiring Moses keep his hands in the air. Moses, Aaron and Hur helped Joshua win the battle and Joshua made the prayers become a reality.

Prayer is important; but prayer alone is not enough. Prayer must be accompanied by action. (James 2:17).

Holy Spirit showed me something special about this Old Testament victory. Moses was given the revelation of the Covenant-Keeping God as Jehovah Nissi – The Lord our Banner. He showed me that over me and every believer is an invisible spiritual banner that every invisible spiritual being can see. It says: "Nick (or, in your case, whatever your name is) is a Winner. Signed, God."

The Banner of the Lord over you says: You are a Winner. Signed, God

The second meaning of the Lord our Banner is found in the Song of Solomon.

> ... his banner over me is love.
> Song of Solomon 2:4 ISV

Holy Spirit revealed to me that on the other side of the spiritual banner that God has placed over every believer are the words "I love Nick (or, in your case, whatever your name is). Signed, God."

The Banner of the Lord over you says: I love you. Signed, God

This is true of every Christian, and in fact of every human who has ever lived. It was this love that motivated God to send His Only Son, Jesus, to the Cross for each and every one of us.

Of course, just as in normal relationships, it is up to every individual to respond to the love that is shown to them. I said "yes" to God's love by putting my trust in Jesus Christ as my Lord and Saviour. Have you?

You can do so by praying this prayer:

Lessons From My Dog

Lord God All-Mighty, I thank You for loving me. I thank You for sending Jesus to pay the price for my sins. I confess my sins and ask Your forgiveness for them. I ask Jesus to come into my life as Saviour and Lord. I receive my salvation by faith in the Lord and in Your Word. I commit myself to follow Jesus and obey Your Word for the rest of my life. Amen.

The Lord's Banner Over You

What is one thing you have learned from this teaching?

What is one thing you can do to implement this teaching?

Faith Declaration:

I thank You Father God for loving me so much that You sent Jesus to suffer, die and triumph over death and Satan, so I could have a good life on earth and throughout eternity with You. I praise You for putting a spiritual banner over my head that says I am a winner. I declare that I shall win in life's challenges, tests and battles because You are with me and for me as I walk with You. I rejoice in the fact that You love me always, not based on my performance, but purely by Your grace. Thank You for loving me first, faithfully and eternally. Lord, I love You in return.

22 — *Being Led by* **Holy Spirit**

For all who are being led by the Spirit of God, these are sons of God.
Romans 8:14 NAS

In this chapter I am sharing with you some principles I have learned over the years as I have developed my own walk with the Lord, my own capacity to hear His voice and the prophetic ministry He has given me.

(i) Read your Bible

If you want to hear from God, read your Bible, which was written by Holy Spirit through various servants of God.

Once, while I was reading Ezekiel 12:3 KJV, the Lord told Lynne and me to "remove thy stuff". To us at that time, it meant: "Take your old furniture with you to Brisbane." We had not intended to do that. We were going to buy new furniture when I got a job there. I didn't ever get a secular job in our new city. I was basically full-time in ministry from the day we arrived. We didn't get a full salary for two years. We could not have afforded to buy new furniture. God knew that in advance of our moving interstate.

A number of years ago, God spoke to me through Job 8:5-7 NIV with a message that directed my decision making. Those verses told me what was going to be the course of my life for years to come, starting with a restoration of my ministry as Senior Pastor of Bayside Christian Family (Apostolic) Church.

On the night my dad died, I cried out to God to show me if dad was eternally safe. I turned to my evening Bible reading and straightaway came to Psalm 61:7 KJV. "He shall abide before God forever." Peace flooded my soul. Two friends sang those verses at dad's funeral.

(ii) Be a good son of God.

If you want to hear from God, treat Him with respect. Be a good sheep, not a stubborn, rebellious, do-your-own-thing goat. Tell God as Jesus did: Not my will but Yours be done. Be a good son, not a lazy, selfish, give-it-to-me-now teenager. Yield your spirit, soul and body to Him, as described in Romans 12:1-2 and 6:13. Then, ask the Lord to lead you and reveal His wisdom to you. (James 1:5-8).]

(iii) Believe for the ministry gifts of Holy Spirit

Earnestly desire spiritual gifts, both for yourself and to hear from God through mature, anointed Christians, who are experienced in operating such gifts, especially prophecy. (1 Corinthians 12:31 and 14:1).

(iv) Ask God questions.

Practice prayer journaling and expect God to answer you, because prayer is a two-way conversation of worship, intercession and listening, not a one-way dump-all-your-troubles-on-God session. You can and should ask the Lord questions about your own life and about people He wants you to minister to.

(v) Understand God is sovereign about what and when He speaks.

Be aware that God doesn't say more than He has to or speak as often as we might like Him to. Sometimes He is like the voice on your GPS, which tests your faith in its previously given directions by times of silence.

(vi) Obey what God last revealed to you.

If you want to hear the next thing God has in mind to say, first obey the last thing He said.

(vii) Learn to discern between the three inner voices you hear.

It would be easy if God spoke like Texan, the devil or like a mafia don or any voice so different from your own that you could immediately tell which voice was God, which was self and which was the evil one.

The problem stems from the fact that we are created as a tripartite being of spirit, soul and body, just like God, the three-in-one Divine Trinity. God speaks to us like deep calling to deep, as the Psalmist wrote. (Psalm 42:7a). He is Spirit and He speaks to our spirit. The devil is also a spirit-being. He too speaks to our spirit.

When these two spirit-communications are given to us, they have to be transferred into our soul in order for us to comprehend them. Sadly, when they arrive in our soul, they have lost their distinct "accent". They sound and feel just like our own thoughts.

Through intimacy of relationship with the Lord and knowledge of His Word, we learn which is the Voice of God and which is the devil and which is just us.

Developing your intimacy with the Lord and your knowledge of His Word equips you to discern God's Voice

---

The content and impact of the message is a good guide to its source. If it's positive and biblical, it's probably God. If it's negative and produces bad feelings inside you like fear or anger or jealousy, then it's going to be the devil.

If it's you and it's positive, step out in faith anyway. If it's you and it's negative, ignore it. Rather, focus on the positive things of the Word, such as Paul advised in Philippians 4:8.

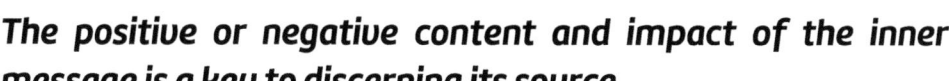

The positive or negative content and impact of the inner message is a key to discerning its source.

18 ways that God speaks

In my book, *You Can Prophesy – Supernatural. Simple. Safe.* I included a chapter listing 18 ways in which God speaks.

(1) The Quickened Word from the Bible. Many will understand this as receiving a "rhema" from the "logos".

(2) Journaling.

(3) The Still Small Voice, which means thoughts and words that come into your mind, which may be quite faint. 1 Kings 19:12. The "still, small voice" is probably the most usual method the Lord uses in communicating with mature ministers.

(4) The Audible Voice of God.

(5) A Dominant, Persistent, Repetitive word, thought or phrase that comes into your mind.

(6) An Inner Witness, an impression, which can be fleeting words, feelings or pictures in your mind.

(7) An Inner Picture that you "see" in your spirit without actually seeing it in your mind.

(8) Conviction, an inner "knowing", that mostly builds within you over time.

(9) Spontaneous revelation, an inspired piece of God's knowledge or understanding.

(10) Vision. This is a clear picture or a video clip that you see with your eyes or in your mind while you are awake. Unless the meaning is very obvious, the vision will require an interpretation, which Holy Spirit will either give to you or to someone else as you share it.

(11) Dream.

(12) Visitation of the Lord or of an angel.

(13) Heavenly revelation. More people than ever before are testifying of being taken to Heaven in the spirit (not physically). Many receive revelation from the Lord Himself.

(14) Remembrance. Holy Spirit may remind you of something such as a Bible verse, an illustration, a quote or a testimony.

(15) Revelation. This may be sparked by anything that gets your attention, such as a circumstance, an event, a casual remark, a person's name, or by a "thing".

(16) Spiritual gifts.

(17) Spiritual partnership in prophetic ministry. This can be when spiritual gifts go together.

For example: in healing ministry, the Word of Knowledge and the gift of Faith are partners. In prophetic ministry, Tongues and Interpretation are two gifts of Holy Spirit that are designed to be used in tandem. A third example is that during church meetings, Holy Spirit may inspire you through the contribution of another person.

(18) Prophetic Presbytery. This is when two or more prophets operate together in ministry to people.

If you receive a serious revelation, make sure you get it confirmed by others who are spiritually qualified to discern it.

(viii) Circumstances can confirm God's Will

Sometimes God uses circumstances to confirm His will. I often tell people that if they are feeling led to relocate somewhere, first go to that place for a holiday. See how you feel there. If things line up, such as positive new connections being made or doors opening there or closing where you are, then it is likely you are heading in the right direction.

However, circumstances must be only the confirming, not the decisive factor, in discerning God's Will. There was a boat waiting for Jonah to take him away from where God wanted him to be. That circumstance did not express what the Spirit was saying.

(ix) Persistent prayer will enhance discernment between two alternatives

I have found that if you have two alternatives to pray about, the one that is of God will grow the more you pray and the other will fade, or at least lose its attractiveness. The God-choice will become more appealing and will excite either peace or faith, or both, within you.

The two inner signs of peace in your heart and of excitement that is spiritual and accompanied by rising faith, are key indicators of the Spirit's leading you into the Will of God.

(x) God may choose unlikely people to speak to you

From the account of the false prophet Balaam, we learn that God can speak through a donkey. (Numbers 22:21-31). He can speak through your parents, or your teenager. Your critic might get something right and it could be a word from God for you. Sometimes a person makes a statement during a conversation that you recognise as having Divine application to your situation.

Sometimes, you can be the donkey. I have had the experience that as I have counselled someone, God has spoken to me through my own advice to them. On other occasions, I have made what I call a "prophetic

Lessons From My Dog

blurt". I have said something casual that was like a word from God to the person.

What is one thing you have learned from this teaching?

What is one thing you can do to implement this teaching?

Faith Declaration:

I thank You Lord for giving me Your Holy Spirit as my Teacher, Helper and Guide. I am so grateful that You are a God Who hears, speaks and leads His people. I declare in Jesus' Name that, because I have chosen to walk in God's ways, my steps are being ordered by the Lord. I praise the Lord because I have open access to the Word of God, the Mind of Christ, the Wisdom of God, prophetic gifts and prophetic people. Hallelujah.

23 Forgiveness and Healing
in Psalm 103:1-3

In these few verses of this wonderful Psalm, we see the Good News of the Gospel revealed in the Old Testament in all its glory. We are told to not forget the benefits that come from being a Christian, a believing Christ-follower. They are life-changing, life-enriching benefits. When we are aware of them they stimulate our faith to receive all that God has given to us in Christ and through His suffering, sacrifice and triumph for us.

(i) Receiving the benefits of salvation starts with a whole-hearted relationship with God.

> *Praise the Lord, my soul; all my innermost being, praise his Holy name.*
>
> *Psalm 103:1*

I want you to notice the word "all", which occurs four times in the first three verses of the Psalm. Praise the Lord, all my innermost being. Then, it says, forget not all His benefits. And then, He forgives all my sins, and He heals all my diseases. Isn't that awesome? Give God your all and you will get His all. That's what the little word "all" is telling us, starting right here in verse 1.

Forgiveness and Healing in Psalm 103: 1-3

Give God your all and you will get His all

In Jeremiah 29:13, God says *"you will seek Me and you will find Me when you search for Me with all your heart."* God is far too important for Him to be an "if", "but", or "maybe" or any kind of low priority in your life.

If you want the benefits of Psalm 103 to come true in your life, you must make a commitment, right at the start, in verse 1. You've got to say: "God, I give you my all." Then you will see all the benefits because they flow out of your relationship with and devotion of all your being to the Lord.

This verse also teaches us to praise God at all times. Never blame Him for bad things that might happen. He is good all the time. All the time, God is good. Praise unlocks the power and blessing of God into your life. This was the key given to the barren and desolate woman in Isaiah 54:1-5. She was promised that if she would praise the Lord and act in faith, she would experience far more good than she could ask or think or imagine.

(ii)   Faith and focus are required to receive all the benefits Jesus has purchased for you.

> *Praise the Lord, my soul, and forget not all His benefits.*
> *Psalm 103:2*

There can be a big stumbling block to people receiving these benefits. Our human minds can be so negative. Negativity depletes our faith. Lack of faith robs us of blessing.

Of course, there are those people who are born optimists. Don't you sometimes want to kick them out of the room? Those people who just radiate confidence. Nothing is too hard for them. They say: "Let's just give it a shot, easy-peasy, no problem whatever." Those kind of people, like over-the-top Pollyannas, can be so annoying.

That's because most of us don't think like that. For many people, when bad things happen to them, even a little pinprick of bad, they focus on that, instead of on the good things they have experienced recently. They remember good things as if they were written in water, but bad things as if they were written in stone. The good things that touch their lives are like a quickly fading shadow. They enjoy the moment, but half an hour later, reality bites again.

If something bad happens, negative-minded people think about it the rest of the day, the rest of the week, the rest of the month, maybe even the rest of the year or worst of all, the rest of their lives. The Psalmist is telling us to do the very opposite of that. We are to remember the benefits that the Lord showers upon His people.

So, right here in verse 2, the Psalmist is talking about an attitude to God, an attitude to the Word, an attitude to life, an attitude about yourself and about the quality of your life. Train your mind, so that instead of thinking about something negative that happened to you, whether it was today or twenty years ago, you choose to forget not all these benefits. Decide to focus on the promises of God's Word.

That positive focus will increase your faith and that faith will prepare you to receive the benefits of the Good News of the Word of God. If you don't have an expectation of any benefit or any good thing happening in your life, it isn't going to happen. If you're not expecting something good, if you're not expecting the good plans of God to come to pass in your life, then they are not likely to happen, are they?

Without faith you can't please God. Without faith, you can't receive a miracle. Without faith, you won't get blessed or experience the benefits of God's Word.

Keep your eyes on God and keep believing His promises, no matter what happens around you. Don't forget all His benefits either by neglect, such as by getting too busy with life to read God's Word, or by focusing on negative things.

(iii) The benefit of being forgiven by God and released from the penalty and power of sin.

Who forgives all your sins, ...
Psalm 103:3a

What better people some would be if they really believed this. Sin holds people in an evil grip. It puts guilt and shame on people. It tells people that they're weak and not strong. Sin is an awful taskmaster. It puts people into such a negative quality of life and can even make them sick.

I remember reading a book by Pastor David Yonggi Cho. He told a story of how this young woman came to him for help. She wasn't eating. She was virtually wasting away. Her life was just a misery. As he began to talk and pray with her, she confessed that there was a time in her life when her older sister and brother-in-law had to bring her into their home. While she was living there her brother-in-law forced himself upon her, without her sister's knowledge. This went on for some time. She became so guilt ridden and ashamed, even though it wasn't her fault. She didn't want it to happen, but her brother-in-law forced the situation, and she was left with the consequences of it. She began to physically waste away, as well as internally be so crippled and negative. Both the Bible and medical science acknowledge that there is a relationship between your health and your mental attitude.

Sin can do to you and your physical health the same type of things that happened to that young woman. Sin lets the devil in. Conversely, when you understand that God forgives all your sins, you will have peace, health and joy in your life.

If the Lord so freely gives us His forgiveness, we cannot disagree with Him. If you hang on to your guilt or shame after you have confessed your sins to Him, you are actually acting as if you have a better sense of justice and grace than God Himself does. That is ridiculously wrong.

Let me show you how wonderful God's forgiveness is: Think of His forgiveness being as big as the biggest and deepest ocean, as infinite as His love. Now imagine you are alone with the Lord on an aircraft carrier out in the middle of that ocean. There is no land in sight. Here you are on this big aircraft carrier with all your sins. The Lord is standing next to you and He says: "Look at this ocean of my forgiveness. What sins have you there? Have you a little sin?" "Yes, I have a little sin. Here it is, Lord." "Okay, throw it overboard." You throw it away.

Where's that sin now? It's at the bottom of the sea of God's forgiveness. What about if you had a middle-sized sin? Maybe it's about the size of a briefcase. You throw it into the ocean. Where does it go? Straight to the bottom of the ocean deep.

Now, have you got a big sin? Maybe you've got a big sin – it's as big as an army tank, it's as big as a house, it's as big as a multi-story building. So, you throw that one in. Whoosh, in it goes. Where is it now? It's at the bottom of the ocean of God's forgiveness, with all the rest of your sins.

It doesn't matter if you've got one, two or three sins, or if you have one, two or three thousand sins, or one, two or three million sins. It doesn't matter how big they are, how small they are, how many they are, how few they are; they all go into that ocean and there's not even a ripple, much less an earthquake or a tsunami.

The Bible says that God chooses to remember our sins no more. It's as if you had never sinned. The Bible actually says in the New Testament, that He blots them out. Now, I don't know about you, but when I was a boy, everything was done by hand. There were no Android tablets, Apple iPhones or personal computers.

If I made a mistake writing out a sentence, the teacher said: "Take a ruler and rule a line through the middle of the incorrect word. Then write the correct word next to it." I didn't like the remembrance of my mistake staring me in the face. So, what I used to do was use my pen to completely overwrite the word until it was rendered illegible, being completely and untidily covered in a dark inky cloud. Therefore, any reader couldn't tell what actual mistake I'd made. Unfortunately, there was now a massive blotch on my page. If I was really ashamed of the mistake I'd made, I'd go to the back of the page and I would put another blotch on the back, so that they couldn't read it backwards, from the underside of the page.

These days Bill Gates and Microsoft have come to the rescue of mistake-makers. They remove all my writing sins as if they'd never existed in the first place. Nobody knows what mistakes I've made before I submit my thesis or put my sermon up on the screen.

Both the Old Testament (Isaiah 43:25) and New Testament (Colossians 2:14) talk about God blotting out our transgressions. He doesn't just remove the sin, but He removes the guilt and the shame and the fear of it happening again.

Jeremiah 31:34 tells us that the Lord chooses to not remember our sin any more. He doesn't have amnesia, He simply chooses to switch off His memory of it. You and I must do the same. We need to think like this: "Okay, I did do that. Lord, I ask Your forgiveness. Now that You have chosen to not remember my sin Lord, I'm going to be like You. I'm going to choose not to remember. And if it ever comes up in my mind again, I will say thank You Lord for your forgiveness. I will again choose not to remember it and I will focus my attention on something else."

Christians must learn to not remember their confessed sins, but at the same time, to forget not all the benefits of their salvation, including what it's like to be forgiven and free of sin.

Remember not your forgiven sins. Forget not all the benefits given to you in the Word of God, because of Jesus

How good it is to be enabled to walk with your head held high (Leviticus 26:13) and to have confidence about who you are in Christ and about your future in Him.

How good it is to not think that the negatives of the past are going to dictate the rest of your life. Hallelujah! How good it is to say: "I've been set free. My life is blessed. I'm expecting good things in my life."

Lessons From My Dog

(iv)   The benefit of healing, both physical and internal.

Who heals all your diseases
Psalm 103:3b

Healing applies to all our sicknesses and dis-eases. I believe the Bible teaches and expresses right here that healing is part of our salvation package. Just as you can receive your salvation, your passport to heaven by faith, so you can receive your healing by faith. Before, on and after the cross, Jesus purchased for us both forgiveness of our sin and the healing of our body.

That's what happened when the paralysed man was lowered down through the roof by his four friends, in Mark 2:1-12. What was the first thing Jesus said to him? Your sins are forgiven. Have you ever wondered what kind of sins a paralysed man can commit? It's not like he can go and rob a bank, is it? A lot of sins we commit are in our head and our heart. Things such as anger, jealousy, lust and pride. Then, there is our mouth! How many times have we deserved to have it washed out with soap? Probably there were occasions when mum didn't need to threaten it; we knew we deserved it enough to almost do it ourselves. That's especially true on those occasions when we said things we wished we could take back; but sadly we can't. We can only apologise and ask forgiveness from the person and from the Lord.

Jesus said, "your sins are forgiven", and then He said "you're healed". There can be a relationship and a pattern here. First, you get the sin out of your life and then second, the healing will come. However, it is not a rule, because Jesus ministered healings of all different kinds and miracles to so many people. He never once was conditional in releasing their healings. Not once did He ever say: "There is no healing for you. God wants you to be sick." Not once did He ever say: "You've been naughty too often." Not once did He say: "It's not your time to be healed."

Jesus gave absolutely unconditional healing to every person, good or bad, young or old, big problem or small problem. Whatever is your need, come to Jesus for this benefit of the Gospel. He says to you: "Out of the grace that is upon Me, out of the goodness of God that is within Me, out of the power of God that flows through My life, be healed, no questions asked, no conditions."

This is the good news. You've got to expect good news in your life, right now, this year. Say to yourself and before the Lord on His throne of grace: "In Jesus' Name I'm going to be healthy this year, I'm going to be healed this year."

Over the years, I have ministered many prayers of healing and seen a number of memorable healings. One was a girl with a broken leg, who was healed in our Church one Sunday morning. The young girl had some soft bone problems previously in her medical history. She came hurtling round a corner and ran into the friend whom she was chasing, who had stopped suddenly. When she ran into her friend, she broke her leg. That was the medical opinion, both of her mother, who was a nurse, and the mother of the other girl, who was also a nurse. They looked for Dr. Luke, who was a valued member, leader and preacher in our church at that time. He has now planted a church elsewhere in Brisbane. He had already left church that morning, so they asked me to come and pray.

The young girl was so embarrassed, she didn't want me there. She was lying on the ground, with the blood drained from her face and her leg swollen, but not penetrated by the bone. So I prayed a short healing prayer for her and left that area of the church fairly quickly. I can't say to you that I had this incredible miracle working faith. I just did what the Bible said.

Five minutes later I was out having coffee with some other people and the mother and daughter walked out to the car.

On the Tuesday, the young girl got her pain back in her leg. Her mother said, "What happened on Sunday? Jesus healed you, didn't He?" "Yes Mum." "All the pain went didn't it?" "Yes Mum." "And the swelling went down?" "Yes Mum." "So, this is just the devil trying to put it back on you isn't it?" "Yes Mum." "Well, we're not going to let him do that are we?" "No Mum." "So we're going to tell the devil to get the hell out of your body and our family." They did that and the pain never came back. As I understand it, she has not had a soft bone issue since then.

Lessons From My Dog

Whether it's a sickness or an accident or if it's hereditary, there's no limit on what God can do.

What is one thing you have learned from this teaching?

What is one thing you can do to implement this teaching?

Faith Declaration:

I thank You Lord for all the benefits Your Word promises me and Jesus purchased for me. Lord, You gave me Your all and I now declare that I give you my all, not out of compulsion or even my desire to be blessed, but because I love You and that is because You first loved me. I ask You to forgive my sins and wash me clean, blotting out my iniquities. Create in me a pure heart, a right and loyal spirit and a willing attitude, in Jesus' Name. Amen. I declare according to Your Word that I am the righteousness of God in Christ, a saint not a sinner. I thank You for my healing and I command my body to be fully and permanently healed, because by the wounds of Jesus I am healed. I ask You Lord to manifest that healing in my body now, in Jesus' Name. Amen.

24 Freedom from Depression; Satisfaction and Renewal in Psalm 103:1-5

In the first three verses of this Psalm, as described in the previous chapter, we are told to remember and be grateful for all the benefits of our relationship with God. These benefits start with salvation and the forgiveness of our sins. They include our healing, both internally and physically.

There was a television salesman on Australian television some years ago, whose key marketing phrase, which became a by-word in our nation, was: "But wait; there's more."

Psalm 103 is like that. These first few verses do not describe the full range of benefits of this Psalm. The rest of the Bible adds lots more benefits that are the inheritance of the born-again children of God.

(i) The Lord can lift you out of depression

Who redeems your life from the pit
Psalm 103:4a

Freedom from Depression; Satisfaction and Renewal in Psalm 103: 1-5

I'm not sure that there has ever been a more stressed and/or depressed generation than this generation. We create our own depression by over-spending. Some people are motivated to "keep up with the Jones'". They get into credit card debt which they are unable to pay. Some people in lower socio-economic circumstances see others on television enjoying benefits they don't have and if they can't access more finance or more credit, they either get angry that the financial gap between people is so wide or they get depressed about what they don't have.

Secondly, there is so much, too much, divorce. In previous generations, there wasn't so much divorce. People didn't say: "I'm married until it gets too tough"; or "I'm married until I can't be bothered anymore"; or "I'm married until I find someone else that I'm more interested in". It wasn't like that. Marriage was respected as the covenant that it is. Men and women stuck with the covenant and they worked through their issues.

My wife and I had issues. We were separated 3 times in the first 5 years. Then we found the Lord and discovered all the benefits of loving, believing in, obeying and serving Him. Lynne has kept me in line for another 40 years since then and we are both happy together.

Of course, divorce has serious negative emotional and financial consequences. It is a big contributor to depression in society among men, women and children.

There are also people who over-prioritise their work and live in stress. This is the way society is geared today. Both parents have to go out and work, and they have to work long and hard, in order to keep up with the mortgage, the costs of education and to live a modern lifestyle that includes having an array of expensive gadgets.

But we can have a peace. In Philippians 4:6-7, the Bible says, prayer can produce a peace that passes understanding. A peace that's beyond the logic of our circumstances. A peace that's beyond the logic of what is going on in the world, and beyond the negative things that people are saying. You can have an inner peace.

The Lord can lift you up out of depression. He can lift you up out of fear. He can lift you up out of negativity.

Lessons From My Dog

I had a crazy upbringing and it was made worse by the fact that I was born with a tendency towards a pessimistic attitude to life. Over all these years of living with the Lord, my "bent" has changed from leaning the wrong way to standing up and leaning in the Lord's way, the right way, the faith way, the love way, the truth way. The tree of my life has put down roots in God and roots in the Word of God. The Lord has changed me from the inside out. He has produced in me faith and love and wisdom and courage and strength. He has given me what I need to succeed in life and to help others succeed also.

I can tell you that if He can bend my tree, He can bend yours. The Lord can lift you up out of that pit and He can put you in a place of confidence and strength and joy and peace. The Good News of the Gospel and this Psalm is that God wants to do that.

Think about this illustration: Imagine that every person in the world can handle 100 units of stress. There are 2 sources of stress, internal and external. Now, imagine you have 85 units of internal stress? This is created by such things as sin, fear, guilt, shame, depression, unresolved issues, resentments, offences, prejudices, problems with rejection and so many other problems bottled up inside of you. There are 85 of your stress units already filling up your capacity tank. You can only handle 15 stress units from the outside world.

This is why for some people, just a small thing can set off a massive reaction. Why? Not because of the size of the small thing, but because they've got too much internal stress, and they can't handle even a small amount of extra pressure or negativity. Whereas, for another person who doesn't have all that internal stress, it's just a pinprick. He doesn't even notice it and certainly doesn't worry about it or waste time and energy being angry about it.

The more internal stress you have, the less outer stress you can handle

Freedom from Depression; Satisfaction and Renewal in Psalm 103: 1-5

If you receive God's love and forgiveness and grace and if you love God and let God truly be Lord of your life and let Him touch you in spirit, soul and body, then your stress units internally will go down. Your peace and courage and strength and faith and love units will go up. You will be able to handle more of the pressure of life even if nothing external changes. You will be able to handle life better. This is what God does for you and with you and in you.

(ii) God doesn't only deal with your negatives, He pours the positives into your life

Who crowns you with love and compassion
Psalm 103:4b

This verse paints the image in me of God being there with you, bringing His infinite supply of everything good to you. He's pouring it out over your life. It's not because you deserve it. It's just that He's got too much. His heart is too full of love and kindness and generosity to keep it all to Himself, so He's got to give it away to anyone who wants what He's got.

It's as if God is saying in these verses: "Look, I've got this never-ending supply that I want to give away. Do you want some? I have more than enough for all.

This is what Grace is. Grace is God doing it out of the goodness of His heart, not because we earn it or deserve it, because we cannot do either. Will you allow God to fill you?

Jesus was often moved by compassion to do miracles. The Lord can do miracles in your life just because He wants to; just because He has compassion for you and your life's circumstances; just because He wants you to have a better life.

When I think about the word "compassion", I also think about this contrast: justice is when we get what we deserve; mercy is when we do not get what we deserve; grace is when we get what we do not deserve.

The problem is that too many people want justice for other people and grace for themselves. You can't do that. You've got to be a person who's willing to express grace towards others, if you want to receive grace, because God gives more grace to the humble. (James 4:6).

***

Justice is when we get what we deserve. Mercy is when we do not get what we deserve. Grace is when we get what we do not deserve.

***

(iii) God does more for His people than meet their bare necessities.

Who satisfies your desire with good things
Psalm 103:5a

The first verse of the great shepherd Psalm 23 tells us that when the Lord is our shepherd, we shall not want. That does not mean God keeps His sheep on survival rations. Neither does Jesus' statement about praying for our daily bread in the famous "Our Father" prayer that He taught His disciples. That part of the prayer is symbolic of us asking God to provide all we need to succeed in life and in service for and with Him to bless others.

Our wonderful, loving, kind, rich and generous Father God wants to freely give us every good gift and especially His Holy Spirit. The following verses should convince you and give you faith to believe that God wants to bless you in lots of ways that are above and beyond your survival needs.

> *⁹ "Which of you, if your son asks for bread, will give him a stone?¹⁰ Or if he asks for a fish, will give him a snake?¹¹ If you, then, though you are evil, know how to give good gifts to your children, how much more will your Father in heaven give good gifts to those who ask him!*
> *Matthew 7:9-11*

"Which of you fathers, if your son asks for a fish, will give him a snake instead?^{12} *Or if he asks for an egg, will give him a scorpion?*^{13} *If you then, though you are evil, know how to give good gifts to your children, how much more will your Father in heaven give the Holy Spirit to those who ask Him!"*
Luke 11:11-13

The young lions lack food and suffer hunger, but they who seek (inquire of and require) the Lord [by right of their need and on the authority of His Word], none of them shall lack any beneficial thing.
Psalm 34:10 AMP

For the LORD God is our sun and our shield. He gives us grace and glory. The LORD will withhold no good thing from those who do what is right.
Psalm 84:11 NLT

Delight yourself in the Lord and He will grant you the desires of your heart.
Psalm 37:4

It is important for me to highlight here the greatest desire of all. That is the desire to go to Heaven. Everyone wants to go there. Well, God says you can. But if you knock on Heaven's door in your own name, you won't get in. So when I go knocking on Heaven's door, I'm not going to say "Hey God, it's Nick!". What I am going to say is "Hey God, I'm here in the name of Jesus. My name is Nick". And the Lord or His angel will say: "Yeah, sure, come on in."

You can only get into God's Heaven – and remember it's His home and we need His permission to enter there – through Jesus. He is the only door. (John 10:7,9). Jesus is the only way. (John 14:1-6; Acts 4:12). There's no back way. There's no climbing through windows. There's no bribing the door-keeper. There's just one door and Jesus is that door. And Jesus satisfies your desire to go to heaven.

When I was a teenager, I lost the impossible-to-lose job. I went out gambling and partying of a night and turned up to work late and had too many days off. My own immaturity and stupidity cost me dearly. Around that time I felt purposeless. I remember asking myself: "What am I meant to do with my life?" I thought: "Maybe I'm on earth to do something bad, like blow up a bank." I don't know why I thought of blowing up a bank; but that's what I thought. Then I thought: "I don't want to blow up a bank! I don't want to do anything horrible like that." I don't believe any right-minded person, teenager or not, deliberately wants to hurt other people or their own or their family's reputation by doing things like that.

I was in a real quandary because I couldn't think of anything positive to do with my life. I did want to be a teacher and I did win a teacher's scholarship, but I was manoeuvred out of that opportunity. So, I went on to become an accountant and thus was born the worst accountant the world has ever seen. (I do hope that is an exaggeration).

Inside, I still wanted to be a teacher. Eventually the Lord brought me to a place where I became a Bible teacher. Along the way I did become a teacher of accountancy as well. So, God was able to satisfy my deep inner desire, a desire He put in my DNA, to teach. Although I was blocked in certain ways and for a number of years, eventually God, when I gave him full control of my life, bought me to that inner satisfaction. He will do the same for you. He will satisfy your life with good things.

In Romans 12:1-2, the Bible says when you put your life as a living sacrifice on the altar for Him and you renew your mind by the Word of God, He will bring you into the will of God that is good and perfect and acceptable for you. The plan of God for your life is good. It will bless you. It'll be something enjoyable. It will be acceptable to you. It's something you're going to be happy about and it's something that's absolutely perfect for you. That's what God does. He brings you into that satisfying of your deep desires with good things.

Freedom from Depression; Satisfaction and Renewal in Psalm 103: 1-5

(iv) The Lord restores or makes up for what you have lost.

Who satisfies your desire with good things so that your youth is renewed like the eagle.

Psalm 103:5b

I'm so grateful that God can turn the clock back on anything. The first promise my wife and I ever got, came when Lynne was out in the garden. We were very new Christians – just a few weeks old in the Lord. Lynne was pottering around out there and this thought came strongly, clearly and repeatedly into her mind. "Joel. Joel. Read Joel."

Lynne thought: "What is that about?" Then she got the idea that maybe there's a book named Joel in the Bible. That's how new in the Lord we were; we just didn't know. So Lynne came inside and she opened the Bible, looked through the index and sure enough, she found a book named Joel. She started reading the book of Joel and she came across this promise (2:25): The Lord will restore the years the locust has eaten.

We had wasted years, not only in our relationship, but in other ways, including financially. Now God was telling us by His Spirit and through His Word that He would restore everything we had lost in every area of life. WOW. What a promise. What a God. Over the following years that we have walked with Him, the Lord has more than restored what we lost. He has lifted us to new heights of being blessed and being a blessing to others.

God can turn the clock back in your life. Whatever you've lost you can get back, whether it's your health or finance or happiness in relationships. Whatever you've lost or wasted, God can restore it and He wants to. Or He can give you something better in its place. Will you say Amen to Him for your own situation?

There is so much good news in these first few verses of Psalm 103. And there is so much more good news everywhere else in the Bible. God wants you to have it all. That's why He sent His Son.

Jesus got what we deserved, which was punishment; so that we could get what He deserves, which is blessing. This is the good news you should be expecting in your life and family this year and beyond. Can you say Amen?

Lessons From My Dog

If you expect to receive these things from God, you'll receive them. If you don't expect them, you won't.

Jesus got what we deserved, which was punishment; so that we could get what He deserves, which is blessing.

Freedom from Depression; Satisfaction and Renewal in Psalm 103: 1-5

What is one thing you have learned from this teaching?

What is one thing you can do to implement this teaching?

Faith Declaration:

I thank You Lord for the amazing good news in your word that is all there for me, because of what Jesus did for me. I thank You Lord for giving me victory over stress and depression, so I can live in Your peace and Joy. I thank You for wrapping me in Your love and overflowing me with Your goodness and grace. I praise You for satisfying my wants and deep desires, as well as my daily needs. I give You glory for restoring all the world, the flesh and the devil have taken from me. I speak abundant restoration over my life and family, our finances and future and our ministry, in Jesus' Name. Amen.

25   5 Steps to Forgiving Others

³² Be kind and compassionate to one another, forgiving each other, just as in Christ God forgave you.
Ephesians 4:32

The New Testament clearly teaches in a number of places that forgiving others is not an option for Christians. It is essential. It is essential, not only so that we can be obedient to God, but also for our own inner health, peace and happiness. Refusing to forgive others can hurt our physical, relational and even financial well-being, as well as our spiritual health and relationship with God. Never forget that Jesus said God measures our love by our obedience. (John 14:21).

For some people, forgiveness comes easy. For others, it can be a very difficult thing; it can be something that takes time and is more of a process than an event.

In this chapter and the next, I will explain some of the steps that can help you to forgive others and to subsequently receive the holistic benefits that ensue because you have obeyed and pleased God.

(i)   Ask God to make you willing to forgive.

You have to accept that forgiveness is always about pardoning the guilty, not the innocent.

It helps you to forgive when you realise that people did not intend to hurt you. I was able to forgive my parents and others based on the attitude and prayer of Jesus: *"Father forgive them for they know not what they do."* (Luke 23:34).

My parents did not deliberately hurt me. In fact they did the best they could, given their backgrounds and lack of parental training and support such as modern society affords. However, I felt hurt and knew I needed to forgive them.

(ii) Forgive by faith.

We forgive by faith, because we know it's the right thing to do in the sight of God and it's the right thing to do for our own inner health.

Forgiveness is a choice. We forgive others by faith, not by emotions. Forgiving those who offend us is never easy; but it is a choice we can and should, indeed we must, make. Don't say you can't, when the reality is you won't.

Jesus challenges and empowers us to love our critics, wrong-doers and even our enemies. (Luke 6:35-36). Unfortunately there may be occasions when someone really is deliberately trying to hurt us. Their intentions do not change the Word of God about forgiveness. The Lord always gives us the ability to live according to His Word and example.

In my life, when I have been majorly hurt in a single instance or wrongly-done-by in ongoing ways, I have had to keep on forgiving way beyond the 70 times 7 that Jesus recommended. (Matthew 18:21-22). Over a lifetime, for some people, it might be 70 times 70 times 70. That's around 1,000 times a year, or 20 times a week. How does that statistic compare with the reality of your life?

I acknowledge that some people live in awful circumstances of life, in which forgiveness is required almost at epidemic levels. For them I pray, and ask you to join me, that the Lord rescues them out of such situations and leads them into His good plan for their lives.

If your life is more ordinary, then, I suggest that if you had a thicker skin and didn't take offence so easily, you would have a lot less forgiving to do. Selah.

I have learned to get tough about what comes against me and stay tender in terms of what comes out of me. As I got more mature and more like Jesus (I still have a long way to go), I discovered I had less difficulty with forgiveness. I took less offence. Forgiveness became a natural and mostly easy way of life.

There are some offences that are so hurtful, so serious and so deep that you will have to forgive the person for that one offence many, many times, until it and he or she has no more power over you, over your thoughts and over your feelings.

I learned to forgive such offences and the offender(s) every time the memory came into my mind, until I was healed. I also learned how to accelerate my own inner healing process. Whenever I forgave, I would ask God for and by faith receive my healing and pray a sincere blessing upon my critic, opponent or betrayer.

(iii) Repent of your own bad attitudes and of any part you may have played in the offence happening.

When relationships break down it is rarely ever 90% one person's fault. Many times it might be 60/40 or 70/30.

I love this contrast: Justice is when we get what we deserve. Mercy is when we do not get what we deserve. Grace is when we get what we do not deserve.

Christians must beware of wanting mercy for ourselves, but judgement and justice for others.

Don't justify your unforgiveness, your pride or your wounded ego. Remember two things: (a) You are a sinner too. You have hurt other people. (b) The Scripture warns us about God's attitude toward pride.

> *...(God) gives us more grace. That is why Scripture says: "God opposes the proud but shows favour to the humble.*
> *James 4:6*

I think most of us know that if we refuse to forgive others then God will not forgive us

Forgive us our debts, as we also have forgiven our debtors. For if you forgive men when they sin against you, our heavenly Father will also forgive you. But if you do not forgive men their sins, your Father will not forgive your sins."

Matthew 6:12, 14-15

Jesus gave us a very graphic example of what the severe consequences of stubborn unforgiveness would look like in the Parable of the Unmerciful Servant. (Matthew 18:21-35).

The other thing you need to consider is that unforgiveness allows Satan access into your life to build strongholds from which he can exert controlling influences in your life.

I like to express it this way: Sin lets the devil in. This is why Holy Spirit gave us the following instruction:

"... do not give the devil a foothold"

Ephesians 4:27

If you give the devil a foothold, he will turn it into a stronghold in your life.

If you give the devil a foothold, he will turn it into a stronghold in your life.

There is another reason why we should forgive Christian people who offend us. In the Damascus Road experience in which Paul met the Lord, Jesus said that Paul's persecution was hurting Him. (Acts 9:4-5). Jesus feels the pain of His people. When Christians hurt, whether offender or offendee, Jesus hurts.

Not only that, but we also negatively impact another divine member of the Holy Trinity, namely, Holy Spirit. Ephesians 4:25-32 tells us that He is grieved and therefore quenched by things like unforgiveness and anger that are caused by offences and disputes.

Here is just one specific example of how disunity affects us spiritually.

> *In the same way you married men should live considerately with [your wives], with an intelligent recognition [of the marriage relation], honouring the woman as [physically] the weaker, but [realising that you] are joint heirs of the grace (God's unmerited favour) of life, in order that your prayers may not be hindered and cut off. [Otherwise you cannot pray effectively.]*
>
> *1 Peter 3:7 AMP*

(iv)   Ask God to heal you and keep on asking and praising until you are healed.

> *Cast your cares on the Lord, because He cares for you.*
>
> *1 Peter 5:7*
>
> *The LORD is close to the broken-hearted and saves those who are crushed in spirit.*
>
> *Psalm 34:18*

Sometimes you might write out your feelings, but send the letter to God, not to the person. The prayer ministry of journaling is such a blessing. I felt that my cares were melting away as I wrote, much more than just by saying my prayer to God. It was as if my stress levels went down as the ink flowed out of my pen.

There comes a time when you need to accept your healing by faith and then act in faith by not thinking about it, and not talking about it. This may be the first time you pray or it could be later than that, depending on how serious the wound is.

Don't wait for an apology in order to get healed. Some apologies never come. I recall once that I virtually begged for an apology from another

Christian that I did not receive. I just had to learn how to forgive and be healed without it.

I cannot control the response of the people who have hurt me. Neither can you. Even when you do the right thing, there is no guarantee anyone else will also do what is right according to the Word of God. You can't even guarantee that other Christians will follow the principles of the Word.

(v) Beware of the destructive side-effects of unforgivemess

Protect yourself and others from the destructiveness that unforgiveness works in your own life and through you to others, who catch the virus of your pain and prejudice.

> *See to it that no one misses the grace of God and that no bitter root grows up to cause trouble and defile many.*
> Hebrews 12:15

If you do not deal with the pain you feel, it festers like an inner poison. The more you think about it, the more you re-create the pain you feel and the more negative and self-pitying you get inside. You can become judgmental, angry, resentful, revengeful or seriously depressed.

Resentment and bitterness, the fruits of unforgiveness, act together as prison bars for your soul. They limit you relationally, emotionally and spiritually. They prevent you from functioning to your best potential or ability.

To get control of your feelings, you have to get control of your thoughts. If you need help to achieve this ask for it. Ask qualified, positive, Christian people. Make yourself accountable for getting healed.

Hurt people hurt themselves. A person can make himself physically sick by constantly focusing on negatives. Eventually other people start avoiding those who are too consistently negative. That means loneliness and rejection get added on to their pain.

Lessons From My Dog

If you go on unhealed, you start blaming God, along with the person who offended you in the first place. Where is your spiritual strength then? Where is your faith, joy, peace and love? Who spends time with God when they are blaming Him for their problems? Who believes God is their answer, when they treat the Lord as if He was their problem?

The other thing is that hurt people hurt people. Even though you started as the victim, you are now multiplying the negativity, especially by your tongue. When people are hurt or angry, they can say things that make the situation worse, things they later regret. Effectively they are putting petrol on fire, instead of water. They are spreading the dis-ease.

5 Steps to Forgiving Others

What is one thing you have learned from this teaching?

What is one thing you can do to implement this teaching?

Faith Declaration:

I thank You Lord for sending Jesus to forgive and save me when I was an undeserving sinner. I praise You because just as You enabled Jesus to willingly go to the cross, so You are giving me the willingness to forgive all who have hurt or offended me. Lord I do this now by faith. I repent of my part in the problem and declare You are my Problem Solver and my Healer. Hallelujah. I ask You for healing and the prevention of further hurt. I declare that there will be peace, reconciliation, unity and blessing, in Jesus' Name. Amen.

26   5 More Steps to Forgiving Others

Bear with each other and forgive one another if any of you has a grievance against someone. Forgive as the Lord forgave you.
Colossians 3:13

Understanding that, in Luke 17:1, Jesus said offences were inevitable, we Christians must know how to overcome them. Forgiveness is a most important component of getting that victory and the healing and peace that come with it.

Jesus included in His statement *"woe to anyone through whom they come."* So, we Christians had better be careful to not cause offence or temptation to others.

This chapter outlines the second group of five ways by which we can forgive, be healed of our hurts and go forward with our life and destiny. These five ways are additional to the previous five, not alternatives to them.

(i)   Ask God to help you see things from the other person's point of view. (Philippians 2:4).

This is neither easy, nor automatic to do. It is something you have to choose to do. It is the key point of Jesus' parable of the speck in the other person's eye and the log in our own. (Matthew 7:1-3-5).

5 More Steps to Forgiving Others

Once you can see things from the other person's perspective, it will probably lessen the negativity you felt. You might be more aware of their pain that caused them to lash out at or snub you or put you down.

Regardless of what motivated their behaviour, as Christians we should still operate according to the Golden Rule.

> *Do to others as you would have them do to you*
> *Luke 6:31*

Paul gave some great advice in his letter to the Romans.

> *[17] Do not repay anyone evil for evil. Be careful to do what is right in the eyes of everyone. [18] If it is possible, as far as it depends on you, live at peace with everyone. [19] Do not take revenge, my dear friends, but leave room for God's wrath, for it is written: "It is mine to avenge; I will repay," says the Lord. [20] On the contrary: "If your enemy is hungry, feed him; if he is thirsty, give him something to drink. In doing this, you will heap burning coals on his head." [21] Do not be overcome by evil, but overcome evil with good.*
> *Romans 12:17-21*

(ii)   Ask The Lord to strengthen your resistance to offences.

Some people are way too sensitive. They make mountains out of ant-hills. They take far too long to overcome negative events or hurtful words. You must accept that offences are inevitable and unavoidable.

Life is not all about "me".

Some people are way too sensitive. Life is not all about "me"

Lessons From My Dog

Jesus said that in this world we would have tribulation, but to not worry about that because He had won the victory and He has given us the means to be victorious. (John 16:33; 1 John 5:4). Jesus also said that just as the world and religious leaders persecuted Him, so they would mistreat us, His followers. (John 15:18-21). So the real question is not "why me", but "why not me?"

We really do have to learn how to turn the other cheek without becoming somebody's doormat or victim. We even have to do this within our own family situations. Sometimes you have to raise your teenagers with one blind eye and one deaf ear. In other words, don't react and certainly do not overreact to absolutely everything they say and do that you might consider provocative.

Professional sportspeople and politicians have to learn to ignore criticism and not be angry with their critics, nor allow criticism to damage their performance or their confidence.

One of the important lessons I have taught people is this: divorce your opinion from your ego.

If people disagree with you, it's not an attack on you as a person. They just have a different opinion as to what is the best kind of music to play on the car radio or what is the best colour paint for the office. Even if it is concerning a matter you deem to be serious, you can still disagree without becoming disagreeable.

Our goal should be to give no offence (2 Corinthians 6:3) and take no offence (Proverbs 19:11), unless we are giving the Gospel, which by nature is offensive to some sinners.

Learn to lift up your shield of faith against offences touching your heart. Learn to wear the helmet of salvation to protect your thought life. Take control of your own mind, thoughts and emotions.

Switch your mind off the person and the problem. Think about other people and other things, not always spiritual things, but things that make you happy, that boost your faith.

> *Finally, brothers, whatever is true, whatever is noble, whatever is right, whatever is pure, whatever is lovely, whatever is*

5 More Steps to Forgiving Others

admirable – if anything is excellent or praiseworthy – think about such things.
Philippians 4:8

Don't mope around, getting gloomy. Get out and do something enjoyable with someone. Talk to someone about how you are feeling. There is an old saying: "A burden shared is a burden halved." The person who first said that must have read Galatians 6:2.

(iii)   Ask God sincerely, to really bless the guilty people.

I discovered that with my deep wounds, I did not get fully and permanently healed unless and until I had done this.

We know God looks upon the heart. That is not just the other person's heart but ours as well. I remember a time when I felt I was a victim. I asked God to deal with the person who was making my life a misery. I wanted God to change him or my circumstances, so I could get away from the consistent bombardment of negativity.

You can imagine how surprised I was when the Lord said to me something like this: "Your attitude stinks. Until you stop judging him and leave him to Me and let Me fix you, I won't be changing your situation at all."

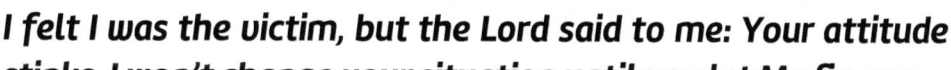

I felt I was the victim, but the Lord said to me: Your attitude stinks. I won't change your situation until you let Me fix you

You must develop the heart of God for others, even your enemies. Your forgiveness must be sincere, "from your heart." (Matthew 18:35).

Sincerely blessing those who have hurt me is the greatest key to healing that the Lord has revealed to me.

Sincerely blessing those who have hurt me is the greatest key to healing that the Lord has revealed to me.

You know you are healed when there is no revenge in your heart or mind, even if you were given the opportunity to take revenge. Joseph did not take revenge on his brothers, nor on General Potiphar or his manipulative wife, nor even the slave-traders who brought him to Egypt, nor anyone in the jail. David twice refused to kill Saul, when he had the king in his power. This is the heart of God. This is Christian forgiveness.

(iv) Do only what God specifically instructs you to in regard to reconciliation

Sometimes people wonder if they should do something tangible to express their forgiveness of the other person. I do not advise that unless and until you get a clear and confirmed (by another wise Christian) witness about exactly what you should do.

There are reasons for this. Firstly, the other person may not even know they have offended you in the first place. I think we all recognise the stupidity of going up to someone and saying: "I didn't like you before, but now I think you're not so bad." Expressing forgiveness to someone for an unknown offence is just a recipe for more heartache.

Secondly, the other person may not receive well, even a good thing that you do. Without judging the other person in your situation, I have known cases where such gestures were like casting pearls before swine – they were not appreciated. According to Philippians 1:9b, discernment is needed even about doing something nice for the other person.

Think about what Paul quoted from Proverbs 25:21-22 to the Romans. He says your good deed will have an impact like that of pouring hot coals on their head. Would you classify that as a pleasant experience? Will they? So, will it produce a positive response? It may better to leave things with

God until the reconciliation is complete. Then wait for an occasion like an anniversary to bless the other person if you wish.

I have learned the hard way that it is best to not write things in a letter or email or text message. Words alone do not convey feelings. They can be too blunt. The other person can read a meaning into them that you never intended. If you feel you absolutely must write something (against my advice), let someone else who is uninvolved read it before you send it.

Some might ask: "Can coffee ever be wrong?" Perhaps not, but it is probably best to leave the coffee as purely a friendship time, not a problem-solving exercise. You might even say when you phone to make the date: "Can we just chat and not talk about anything serious?"

(v) Be a Reconciler (2 Corinthians 5:18-19) and Peacemaker (Matthew 5:9).

> *Do all that you can to live in peace with everyone.*
> *Romans 12:18 NLT*

Of course, there are times when you simply must follow proper conflict resolution and grievance procedures. I don't have time to go into that in this book, but please, especially in church life, use Matthew 18:15-17 as your guide and God's restorative love as your motivation.

Do not let the devil use the offence or hurt or dispute to bring division in the church or disrepute to the Lord and the church in the world. Don't let the problem or issue become an emotional football or time-bomb that divides people into the "our" or "their" camp.

Yes, we have the right and responsibility to receive comfort and advice, but two wrongs don't make a right. If you just want to gossip about (often disguised in the name of a "prayer request") and criticize the person behind their back, then you are doing more damage than what the problem was in the first place. False perceptions and accusations destroy people's lives.

The opposite of reconciliation is stress between people, unhappy emotions, distorted or disrupted communication and things like that. How much better is the Lord's healing, unity and peace. Just look at the rewards such unity brings, as recorded in Psalm 133.

5 More Steps to Forgiving Others

What is one thing you have learned from this teaching?

What is one thing you can do to implement this teaching?

Faith Declaration:

I thank You Lord for enabling me to see and do things as You do. I thank You for causing me to be tough concerning what comes against me and tender regarding what flows out of me. In Jesus' Name, I declare I am wearing the helmet of salvation to protect my thought life and I am lifting the shield of faith against every fiery dart of the world, the flesh and the devil. I decree that I am not easily hurt or offended. I speak Your blessing over those who affected me negatively and declare afresh my forgiveness of them. I thank You for my healing, which I believe is complete and permanent. I ask for wisdom in these and all other relationships and communications. I declare that I have the Mind of Christ and the Wisdom of God to guide me, by the help of Holy Spirit. I thank You Lord for the anointing of reconciliation and peacemaking on my life in Jesus' Name. Amen.

27 What Jesus did at Easter

When he had received the drink, Jesus said, "It is finished." With that, He bowed His head and gave up His spirit.
John 19:30

Then Jesus shouted out again, and he released his spirit.
Matthew 27:50 NLT

Easter is the greatest celebration time of the year for Christians in every nation and every generation. This is because Jesus paid the supreme sacrifice and won the greatest victory – His suffering and triumph changed everything for the better for everyone who will believe.

As Jesus was bleeding and dying on the cross for our salvation, He made some amazing statements. Jesus shouted out His smallest but supremely significant statement just before He yielded up His spirit to the Father.

TETELESTAI – Jesus' victory shout

Jesus shouted a 10-letter Greek word ("tetelestai") which is translated in John 19:30 by three (3) simple English words, namely, "it is finished".

Let me point out that Jesus did not cry out, as if in defeat, "I am finished", because He knew He would be raised from the dead on the third day.

What Jesus Did at Easter

On every Easter Sunday, we celebrate His wonderful and supernatural resurrection, which is an absolutely foundational belief to our Christian faith.

Easter is not the mournful memory of the death of a loved one. It is the celebration of our Saviour and Lord, Jesus Christ, Who shouted out victoriously "'it' is finished!"

When Jesus was on that cross, He was not filled with self-pity and despair. Yes, He did cry out to His Father that He felt forsaken (Matthew 27:46), but we were on Jesus' mind. Our salvation and reconciliation to God and eternal sonship with Him were the joy that was set before Jesus that enabled Him to endure the cross, despising the shame of being crucified as a common criminal. (Hebrews 12:2).

Jesus did not cry out in self-pity or defeat. He shouted out victoriously "It is finished." The price was paid for salvation and every blessing and every promise in the Bible to become a reality in the lives of all believers.

I like the saying: "It was love, not nails, that kept Jesus on the cross." We should return His love, by demonstrating our love for him.

> *And He died for all, that those who live should no longer live for themselves but for Him Who died for them and was raised again.*
> *2 Corinthians 5:15*

Let me ask this question on your behalf: "What was the 'it' that was finished?"

Lessons From My Dog

We have a clue to the answer to this question in John's Gospel chapter 17 and verse 4. Jesus is praying to the Father just before He was arrested and sentenced to death.

> *I have brought You glory on earth by completing the work You gave Me to do.*
> *John 17:4*

So, what was the chief work the Father sent Jesus to Earth to do?

> *For the Son of Man came to seek and to save what was lost.*
> *Luke 19:10*

Jesus' primary purpose was to bring salvation to mankind, by reconciling the human race to God. To do this, He had to satisfy all the demands of the religious law and pay the penalty for our sins, past, present and future.

Warren Wiersbe is a pastor, author and theologian who researched this Greek word "tetelestai." He discovered that it was commonly used by people in a variety of occupations, back in Bible times.

Meaning of Tetelestai – Jewish priests

One of the duties of the Jewish Priests was to examine the animals which the people brought to offer to God either as sacrifices for their sins or as thanksgiving for His blessing. Their religious laws disallowed any animals that were blemished in any way.

> *[6] "A son honors his father, and a servant his master. If I am a father, where is the honor due Me? If I am a master, where is the respect due Me?" says the Lord Almighty.*
>
> *[8] "When you bring blind animals for sacrifice, is that not wrong? When you sacrifice crippled or diseased animals, is that not wrong? Try offering them to your governor? Would he be pleased with you? Would he accept you?" says the Lord Almighty.*

[13] "When you bring injured, crippled or diseased animals and offer them as sacrifices, should I accept them from your hands?" says the Lord. [14] "Cursed is the cheat who has an acceptable male in his flock and vows to give it, but then sacrifices a blemished animal to the Lord. For I am a great king," says the Lord Almighty, "and My Name is to be feared among the nations."

Malachi 1:6a, 8, 13b, 14

After the priest had examined their sacrifice, he would say (the Hebrew or Aramaic equivalent of the Greek word Tetelestai): "It is perfect"... "it is finished" ... "it is complete." In other words, it's all there, nothing is missing, the animal is suitably unblemished for the sacrifice.

Jesus Christ, who died on the Cross for us was God's perfect, unblemished, sinless, faultless sacrifice. John the Baptist called Him *"the Lamb of God, Who takes away the sins of the world"* (John 1:29).

On the Cross, Jesus finished the work of Reconciliation, Redemption and Salvation.

Meaning of Tetelestai – Merchants

Businessmen in Jesus' day also used the equivalent of the Greek word "tetelstai." To them, it meant "the debt is fully paid." If you had purchased something, the merchant would take your money and then would give you a receipt. That receipt would say "tetelestai – it is finished." The debt has been fully paid.

As sinners, you and I are in debt to our Holy God and, like the debtors in Jesus' parable (Matthew 18:23–35), we cannot pay this debt. We have broken God's law. We are spiritually and morally bankrupt. Jesus came and paid the debt for us. That is what tetelestai means.

> *You know the Grace of our Lord Jesus Christ, that though He was rich, yet for your sake He became poor, that you through His poverty might become rich.*
>
> *2 Corinthians 8:9*

> *For even the Son of Man did not come to be served, but to serve, and to give his life as a ransom for many.*
>
> *Mark 10:45*

> *For there is one God and one mediator between God and men, the man Christ Jesus, who gave himself as a ransom for all men.*
>
> *1 Timothy 2:5,6*

Jesus ransomed us. He paid our Spiritual and Moral Debt in full. He became poor for us so that we could become spiritually and morally rich in the sight of God through Him.

Praise God, we were kidnapped by the devil through our sin and the Lord paid the ransom for us to be forgiven and set free. He paid that ransom to God, not the devil. God then commanded the devil to free believers.

Praise God, we committed spiritual crimes, but Jesus paid the fine that was accepted by the court of Heaven.

Jesus is the Perfect Sacrifice Who was punished for our sins so that we could experience God's loving Mercy and Grace instead of His Holy Judgment.

Jesus got what we deserved, which was punishment, so we could get what He deserves, which is blessing.

A famous Bible teacher and pastor from the 17th century, Matthew Henry, wrote a 6-volume verse-by-verse commentary on the entire Bible. In it he wrote that the death and triumph of Jesus purchased 4 things: i. Full satisfaction for sin; ii. Fatal blow to Satan; iii. Fountain of Grace that will flow forever; iv. Foundation of Peace that will last forever.

What Jesus Did at Easter

Meaning of Tetelestai – Artists

According to Warren Weirsbe, a third group of people who used the expression "tetelestai" was artists. When a painter had put the final touches on his work, he would step back and say: "Tetelestai – it is finished!" He meant: "My picture is completed."

In other words, the concept the artist had in his mind when he began the painting was now a reality on canvas for all to see.

The Old Testament is full of prophecies about, and symbols of, the Plan and Purposes of God. They described the plan of salvation that God had in mind and which Jesus fulfilled. Two well-known examples are: (a) the sacrificial offering of his son Isaac by Abraham – Jesus was God's Son, who was sacrificed for the forgiveness of our sins; and (b) the prophetic act of Moses striking the Rock to release life-giving water for the people of God. Jesus was struck through His suffering and death on the Cross, so that believers could find new life in Him.

The first prophecy of Jesus and what He would do occurred right back in the Garden of Eden, after the sin of Adam and Eve. God said to the devil, the Offspring of the woman "...will crush your head and you will strike His heel". (Genesis 3:15). Jesus fulfilled this prophecy.

In the last twenty-four hours of His life, Jesus fulfilled 16 Messianic prophecies. Some of those prophecies were: He would be betrayed by a friend; the betrayal price would be thirty pieces of silver; He would be silent before His accusers; He would be crucified with criminals and yet buried in a rich man's tomb; He would be scourged and His body pierced, but none of His bones would be broken; His executioners would cast lots for His clothing.

Various authors, including Herbert Lockyer, have written that the mathematical possibilities of one man fulfilling each and every one of these prophecies in any time frame, or of the fulfillment being a co-incidence, happenstance or an accident are 1 in 537 million (537,000,000)

Arthur T. Pierson used an illustration similar to this:
It would be as likely as if a single drop of water in the ocean was coloured bright red and a blind-folded child with a bucket was taken out to a

random spot and drew out sea-water that included the only drop of red water in the entire ocean.

Another author quoted a scientist, Peter Stoner, as suggesting that the possibility of just 8 prophecies being fulfilled by Jesus were 1 in a hundred thousand million million (100,000,000,000,000,000). This would be similar to covering the entire land area of Australia with our large silver 50-cent pieces stacked 10-15 coins high. Imagine one of those coins was dyed red and submerged somewhere in that ridiculously impossible-to-count stack of coins. What would be the possibility that a prospector, with just one plunge of his arm anywhere in Australia, grasped hold of that exact red coin?

It is mathematically impossible for the prophecies Jesus fulfilled to be coincidental. He supernaturally fulfilled the previously declared Word and Will of God. Therefore mathematics proves that God is God, that the Bible is true and that Jesus is Lord.

It is mathematically impossible for the prophecies Jesus fulfilled to be coincidental. He supernaturally fulfilled the previously declared Word and Will of God. Therefore mathematics proves that God is God, that the Bible is true and that Jesus is Lord.

The wonderful thing which follows on from this is that every prophecy and promise of God in the Bible is also true. Because you belong to the Lord, then every prophecy and promise of God in the Bible is true for you. By faith you can experience the reality of every promise of God in your life. This includes salvation, healing, peace from strife, reconciliation from division, prosperity for your labour, investing and giving, freedom from every negative thing that has held you back etc.

Meaning of Tetelestai – Victory in Battle

Author Malcolm Smith discovered a fourth use of the word "tetelestai." It was shouted by a Roman general when he saw that the enemy had been defeated.

> *When you were dead in your sins and in the uncircumcision of your flesh, God made you alive with Christ. He forgave us all our sins,* [14] *having cancelled the charge of our legal indebtedness, which stood against us and condemned us; He has taken it away, nailing it to the cross.* [15] *And having disarmed the powers and authorities, He made a public spectacle of them, triumphing over them by the cross.*
>
> Colossians 2:13-15

> *He who does what is sinful is of the devil, because the devil has been sinning from the beginning. The reason the Son of God appeared was to destroy the devil's work.*
>
> 1 John 3:8

So, Jesus came to destroy the power of sin and to set people free from the grip of the devil and from every form of darkness, evil and negativity in their lives.

> *The thief comes only to steal and kill and destroy; I have come that they may have life, and have it to the full.*
>
> John 10:10

Just as you and I have our own natures, it is the nature of God to love, to do good, to heal and to forgive. That's just the way He is. It is the nature of the devil to do harm and evil.

God loves people. Conversely, the devil hates people because we are made in the image of God, even if it is an image damaged by sin. A dirty, wrinkled, even torn $20 dollar note is still recognizable and valued as a $20 dollar note.

Lessons From My Dog

I'm reminded of the story about the scorpion and the turtle. The scorpion wanted to cross the river, but he couldn't swim. So he asked the turtle for a ride. But the turtle said, "Oh no. I can't take you on my back because if I do, you'll sting me." And the scorpion replied, "Oh no. I give you my word. I won't sting you."

The turtle, with some persuasion, finally agreed and let the scorpion get on his back.

They set out across the river together and when they had reached about the middle, the scorpion could resist no longer.

He reached underneath the shell and stung the turtle. As they began to slowly sink to the bottom, the turtle cried out: "But you promised; you promised you wouldn't sting me."

The Scorpion replied, "Yes, I know I promised. But I couldn't resist. You see, it's my nature to sting."

It's God's nature to love, to forgive, to give, to bless, to help, to heal and to empower. It's the devil's nature to hate, to accuse and offend, to steal, to curse, to hinder, to hurt and to destroy. The devil uses things such as sickness, strife and discouragement; but, sin is his chief weapon, his deadliest sting.

It was only by the sacrificing of His own sinless and wholly positive life that Jesus could make salvation available to us, in spirit, soul, body and quality of life.

You must have the confidence that Jesus has paid the price which purchased every blessing you will every need in any and every area of your life. This is what 2 Corinthians 1:20 means! Jesus said "yes" to every promise in the Bible, whether it is for salvation, reconciliation to God and man, healing, renewal of your mind, financial blessing, career advancement, leadership influence in the seven so-called mountains of society (Family, Church, Government, Education, Business, Media, Arts/Sport/Entertainment).

So, healing belongs to you. Promotion belongs to you. Spiritual gifts belong to you ... all because of Jesus! Hallelujah.

What Jesus Did at Easter

The other area in which you must exercise faith is by taking up your authority in Christ to defeat the devil in your own life and family and to destroy his works in others as you minister to them in the Lord's Name.

> *Behold! I have given you authority and power to trample upon serpents and scorpions, and [physical and mental strength and ability] over all the power that the enemy [possesses]; and nothing shall in any way harm you.*
> *Luke 10:19 AMP*

By faith accept that Jesus has paid the price for every blessing and every promise in the Bible to become a reality in and through your life. By faith accept that Jesus has given you His delegated authority and power to be victorious in every area of your life.

Through Jesus and because of Him, you can be victorious over sin. Through Jesus and because of Him, you can be victorious over sickness. Through Jesus and because of Him, you can be victorious over guilt, shame, fear, anger, lust, greed, depression, confusion and every negative force within you. Through Jesus and because of Him, you can be victorious over addictions and every bad habit that afflicts your life, including bad relational behavior that is motivated by rejection and other dysfunctional issues. Through Jesus and because of Him, you can be victorious over generational problems. Through Jesus and because of Him, you can be victorious over poverty. Through Jesus and because of Him, you can be victorious over all the works of the devil.

By faith accept that Jesus has paid the price for every blessing and every promise in the Bible to become a reality in and through your life ... and that you have His delegated authority and power to be victorious in every area of your life

Conclusion – 7 things that ended and 7 things that started at Easter

There is not room in this chapter to explain the following seven things that Jesus finished on the Cross and the accompanying seven things that started with Jesus' resurrection.

(i) It was the end of the God-ordained suffering that Jesus went through on our behalf. And it was the end of His human life, not His humanity, and the end of His laying aside His Deity.

It was the beginning of Jesus' Eternal High Priestly ministry that gives us such confidence, even boldness, before the throne of Grace. Jesus once again took up His place of glorified Lordship at the Father's right hand to speak and act on our behalf.

(ii) It was the end of the dominating power of sin in the lives of believers.

It was the beginning of the power of inner righteousness that God would supply to every Christian through Jesus Christ.

The wonderful truth of the Gospel is that Jesus does not just set us free from the penalty of sin, He releases us from the power of sin, including pornography and other addictions such as alcohol and drugs, which induce so much sin, because people hand over the control of their lives to these negative forces.

(iii) It was the end of the Law and of salvation through obedient, good and religious works.

It was the beginning of both salvation by grace through faith and the Age of New Covenant Grace, which ushered in times of experiencing the limitless unmerited favour and miracle-working enabling power of God, until Jesus comes again to take believers into eternity with Himself.

(iv) It was the end of all the sacrifices and religious rituals whereby man tried to get close to God, to communicate with Him and please Him by religious performances.

It was the beginning of restored relationship with God on a personal basis in which we can each and all experience God, and His Love, so that we fellowship with Him, love, honour, serve and please Him, by faith in Christ and through the power of Holy Spirit.

(v) It was the end of Israel being the primary focus of God's attention.

It was the beginning of the Christian Church taking up their inheritance as the spiritual people of God.

(vi) It was the end of Jesus in His Humanity being able to do the Father's work only in one place, at one time.

It was the beginning of the Age of Holy Spirit, Who would empower a world-wide, world-changing movement of Christian believers who do God's work and continue Christ's ministry on the earth by faith, in His power.

(vii) It was the end of Satan's rule as the god of this world. It was the end of the devil's usurped authority which he stole from Adam, through deception and sin, when he was God's chosen federal head of the human race.

It was the beginning of the restored authority of believers as God's representatives on earth, because Jesus took back what the enemy stole from Adam. Jesus became the second Adam, the new leader of all mankind in the sight of God, the Father's chosen manager of the earth and everyone and everything in it.

3 questions

In response to what you have read in this chapter: (a) Will you ask God NOW to forgive your sins? (b) Will you thank Jesus for what He did for you? (c) Will you ask the Lord for His power to be evident in your life?

What is one thing you have learned from this teaching?

What is one thing you can do to implement this teaching?

Faith Declaration:

I thank You Lord Jesus for taking the punishment for my sins on the Cross. I praise You for rising in triumph over sin, death and the devil. I glorify You for passing Your power, authority and victory on to me, both for myself and my needs and also to minister to others to meet their needs. I declare that I am righteous in the sight of God because of the shedding of Jesus' Blood for me. Therefore the Lord is always ready, willing and able to bless, empower and use me for His glory. I thank you that I am free from the requirements of the Law and from the effort of trying to win the approval of God by my religious performance. I praise You Lord that the curtain in the temple was torn to indicate that I have free access to My Father in Heaven, both to build our relationship and partnership, and to have my prayers answered at the Throne of Grace. I give You praise my God, because You have a limitless supply of un-earned, un-merited grace and enabling power to pour into and through my life. Hallelujah.

28 How to Treat Holy Spirit

But I tell you the truth, it is to your advantage that I go away; for if I do not go away, the Helper will not come to you; but if I go, I will send Him to you.

John 16:7 NAS

What a nonsensical and unwelcome statement of Jesus this must have been to the ears of His disciples. Let's face it, if you had the choice between the visible Lord Jesus Christ, Who went about doing good, healing all those who were sick and oppressed of the devil (Acts 10:38), and a helpful friend of His, Whom would you choose?

However, this is no ordinary friend.

(i) Who is Holy Spirit?

Holy Spirit is an equal member of the Holy Trinity. (Luke 3:21-22; Matthew 28:19; 2 Corinthians 13:14). Holy Spirit is God because He is Eternal, Omnipotent, Omniscient and Omnipresent. Holy Spirit is a Divine Person, not a thing, such as if He was merely "power" like electricity.

How can you make electricity "grieve"? How can a thing be your teacher, guide or helper. You need a Divine Person to be your source of wisdom, healing, righteousness and strength. There is no vending machine that can enrich your life with all the blessings and resources Holy Spirit is commissioned to impart to you from God.

(ii) Holy Spirit is for every Christian

> *³⁸ Peter replied, "Repent and be baptized, every one of you, in the name of Jesus Christ for the forgiveness of your sins. And you wil receive the gift of the Holy Spirit. ³⁹ The promise is for you and your children and for all who are far off — for all whom the Lord our God will call."*
>
> Acts 2:38-39

The wording of this verse tells us that Holy Spirit is for every Christian in every nation and every generation. They may be far off in distance from Jerusalem or far off in time from the apostle Peter, but when the Lord calls them to come to Christ, then the same Holy Spirit is waiting to indwell and fill them the same as He did on the day of Pentecost and in every generation since.

(iii) Holy Spirit represents Jesus and empowers Christians

Firstly, Holy Spirit indwells the Christian representing the Presence of the Father and the Son. He produces the fruit of Christ-likeness in believers.

Secondly, Holy Spirit fills us and empowers us for supernatural living, in which we reproduce the works that Jesus did.

I want to focus on the empowering of Holy Spirit by considering an Old Testament example, David.

> *So Samuel took the oil and anointed David in the presence of his brothers and from that day on the Spirit of the LORD came powerfully upon David.*
>
> 1 Samuel 16:13

> *One of the servants said to Saul, "One of Jesse's sons from Bethlehem is a talented harp player. Not only that — he is a brave warrior, a man of war, and has good judgment. He is also a fine-looking young man, and the LORD is with him." ..... ²³And whenever the tormenting spirit from God troubled Saul, David*

> *would play the harp. Then Saul would feel better, and the tormenting spirit would go away.*
>
> *1 Samuel 16:18,23*

In verse 23, we learn that Holy Spirit enabled David to get rid of Saul's demons by his praise.

It is important to note here that worship attracts the Presence of God, Who drives out demons. Secular music of any generation has no power to repel demons. Some worldly lyrics today actually attract them.

> *David said to Saul, "Your servant has been keeping his father's sheep. When a lion or a bear came and carried off a sheep from the flock, 35 I went after it, struck it and rescued the sheep from its mouth. When it turned on me, I seized it by its hair, struck it and killed it. 36 Your servant has killed both the lion and the bear; this uncircumcised Philistine will be like one of them, because he has defied the armies of the living God. 37 The LORD who rescued me from the paw of the lion and the paw of the bear will rescue me from the hand of this Philistine." Saul said to David, "Go, and the LORD be with you."*
>
> *1 Samuel 17:34-37*

David had been overlooked even by his dad, but he was God's choice to be Israel's next king, because of his heart.

David would not have been overlooked if he had already killed the lion and bear. He didn't do those exploits until after Samuel anointed him and Holy Spirit came mightily upon him. Holy Spirit enabled David to slay a lion and a bear and then a giant.

David was a worshipper in the fields with the sheep for years. After the anointing of Holy Spirit, David's worship was empowered to drive away demons.

> *In everything (David) did he had great success, because the Lord was with him.*
>
> *1 Samuel 18:14*

(iv) How Christians should treat Holy Spirit

(a) Jesus said we must *be "thirsty"* for Holy Spirit and "come and drink".

> *On the last and greatest day of the festival, Jesus stood and said in a loud voice, "Let anyone who is thirsty come to Me and drink. [38] Whoever believes in Me, as Scripture has said, rivers of living water will flow from within them."[39] By this He meant the Spirit, whom those who believed in Him were later to receive. Up to that time the Spirit had not been given, since Jesus had not yet been glorified.*
>
> *John 7:37-39*

We must be thirsty for God (Psalm 42:1,2), not just for an experience. Our thirst must come from our whole heart. (Jeremiah 29:12,13). Then, God is sure to reply. (Luke 11:9-13; James 4:8a).

Let me ask you: "Where are you on the Holy Spirit and Spiritual Gifts continuum?"

- knowledgeable and antagonistic;
- ignorant and antagonistic;
- ignorant and uninterested;
- ignorant but willing to learn;
- knowledgeable and neglectful;
- ignorant and learning;
- open to receiving;
- desiring to receive (i.e. being thirsty);
- committed to receiving, which means desiring and pursuing (i.e. being thirsty and coming to drink);
- learning;
- putting learning into practice by faith;

- zealous with wisdom;
- zealous without wisdom;
- striving;
- faking.

The "thirsting" and "coming" that Jesus talked about means that we must be not merely "open" to receiving Holy Spirit and His empowering, but "committed" to receiving. Holy Spirit is available to anyone and everyone, all the time. Over many years of ministry, I have learned that when a person is spiritually thirsty for this experience, it is a sign that it is not only God's Will for them to receive, but also His Time.

(b) We must *not grieve* Holy Spirit. (Ephesians 4:30).

In the context of this instruction (Ephesians 4:17-5:12) Paul writes to Christians about not grieving the Holy Spirit by doing the works of the flesh. He says I insist that you must not live as the world does. He lists a lot of specific behaviours that do grieve Holy Spirit, including hardness of heart, lust, impurity, bitterness, unwholesome talking and lying.

Paul also writes a number of positive behaviours that attract the empowering of Holy Spirit, such as putting on the new self in Christ, giving to others, forgiving people, showing love and integrity.

Two of the grieving behaviours that I will draw your attention to are, firstly, anger and, secondly, stealing.

> *And "don't sin by letting anger control you." Don't let the sun go down while you are still angry,[27] for anger gives a foothold to the devil.*
> *Ephesians 4:26-27 NLT*

Most of our anger is sinful; it is of the flesh. It's your pride or ego that has been offended; or you have been inconvenienced by someone; or you have suffered wrongfully and been hurt or robbed or betrayed by someone. The Bible here says, regardless of the cause of the anger, you should resolve it in your heart before nightfall.

In terms of other Scripture verses about conflict resolution, you should definitely resolve it in your heart and if possible between people before you next take Communion at church. (Matthew 5:23-24).

Righteous anger is when there is an obvious case of injustice. You may have been the victim or perhaps it was someone close to you. The Bible still says you must not stay angry. You can pursue justice without carrying your anger into the battle. Holy Spirit will help you when you seek to obey this instruction. But if you do not aim to subdue your anger, you will grieve Holy Spirit and then He cannot empower you to overcome it and its negative side effects.

Secondly, we see the stunning transformation Holy Spirit can do in someone's life if they do things God's way.

> *Anyone who has been stealing must steal no longer, but must work, doing something useful with their own hands, that they may have something to share with those in need.*
> *Ephesians 4:28*

What a change of heart this verse represents, as well as a drastic lifestyle change. The thief stops thinking selfishly, as if the world owes him a living. He overcomes whatever internal forces and outward circumstances were pushing him into thievery.

He begins to use his gifts and talents for good, not evil. He wants to make a contribution to the lives of others. He is a living example of God giving more grace, as in 2 Corinthians 9:8.

Another list of things that grieve Holy Spirit is found just before Paul tells us what the fruit of the Spirit is. (Galatians 5:13-25).

To experience the best and long-lasting empowering of Holy Spirit, to build a great life and to leave a lasting legacy, you must build a great character.

Don't be anointed and unholy like secular people who are talented but tainted, such as some famous sportsmen and politicians have been.

To experience the best and long-lasting empowering of Holy Spirit, to build a great life and to leave a lasting legacy, you must build a great character.

If you allow bad things to remain in your life they do not only grieve Holy Spirit, but Ephesians 4:27 says they give the devil the opportunity to attack you. He will turn his opportunity into a foothold and a foothold into a stronghold in your life.

> *... give the enemy no opportunity for slander"*
> *1 Timothy 5:14b*

How much better it is to live so that, if people do talk about you behind your back, it will be good talk.

(c) Do *not resist* Holy Spirit. (Acts 7:51).

Paul, who wrote the advice in Ephesians, learned the hard way to not keep on resisting the Lord. In Acts 26:14, he admitted that Holy Spirit had been prodding him to stop his persecuting behaviour. When Jesus appeared to him, Paul was knocked to the ground and dazzled to such an extent that he didn't see for three days until Ananias prayed for him.

In that Damascus road meeting, Jesus used a word that means ox-goad or cattle-prod. So the promptings of Holy Spirit had not been subtle, but imply that Paul was a strong, stubborn, thick-skinned, stupid bull, who was being hit repeatedly by a long, strong, pointed stick.

The New Testament epistles tell us that our old Adamic, sinful, flesh nature is in opposition to our own regenerated spirit and to Holy Spirit. (Galatians 5:17). Also, our natural man cannot understand the things of the Spirit. (1 Corinthians 2:14). So we must be careful to not slip into a casual spirituality, where we default back to that old nature and find ourselves resisting God.

In Genesis 6:3, the Lord said to an evil world: "My Spirit shall not always strive with man." And that didn't end well for mankind, when the flood came. Only righteous Noah and his family and the animals on the ark survived.

I don't want to frighten you with the reminder of what happened to Ananias and Sapphira when they lied to and put Holy Spirit to the test with their sin. I do not believe that is normal New Testament, New Covenant Christianity.

Neither do I believe that the Lord puts sicknesses on people to get their attention or teach them a lesson. Jesus never did that and He was and is the exact representation of the Father. So, if Jesus didn't do it, then the Father doesn't do it and Holy Spirit doesn't do it.

I do not believe that the Lord puts sicknesses on people to get their attention or teach them a lesson.

However, there are serious warnings in the New Testament concerning "insulting the Spirit of Grace" (Hebrews 10:29) and blaspheming against Holy Spirit (Matthew 12:24-32; Mark 3:22-30), which is saying that something, which is the Spirit's doing, is of the devil.

(d) We are told to *not "quench"* Holy Spirit (Thessalonians 5:19 NIV); nor "stifle" Him (NLT), nor "put out the Spirit's Fire" (ISV).

Sadly, too many Christians do quench Him. For some, it is out of ignorance. They may not have sufficient knowledge about Holy Spirit. Some believers are taught as if the Holy Trinity is Father, Son and Holy Bible. They are not taught about the Personhood of Holy Spirit.

Three common ways by which Christians quench or stifle Holy Spirit or put out His fire are: by disobedience, when we refuse to obey the Word of God or the leading of Holy Spirit; by un-belief, which is not just doubt but the refusal to believe; by letting fear overcome our faith.

Christians quench and stifle Holy Spirit by their disobedience, unbelief and fear

Let me tell you something the Lord Himself revealed to me. It is so simple, yet so powerful: "Every circumstance of fear is also an opportunity for faith."

(e) The best and right way to treat Holy Spirit is to *fan Him into flame* and stir up your gifts. (2 Timothy 1:6,7).

When we spend time with God, worshipping, praying and listening, we give Holy Spirit the opportunity to speak and lead us into the God things He wants to partner with us in to fulfil the Will of God on earth.

When we love, give, speak the Word of God, obey and step out in faith in other ways, we activate Holy Spirit, just as God's voice commands did in Genesis chapter 1. Holy Spirit was there hovering, but He didn't spring into action until God spoke.

You have to do something to stir yourself into action, to stir up your faith and to use the talents, resources, spiritual gifts and opportunities God gives you. Then you will know how real, how holy, how wise, how powerful and how empowering Holy Spirit is.

> *For this reason I remind you to fan into flames the spiritual gift God gave you ....*
> *2 Timothy 1:6 NLT*

Why don't you give God an extra one hour each week? Use half of that hour to be still before God, worshipping, waiting, reading His Word, listening and asking Him questions like: Lord is there anything You want me to do today?

The other half of that hour is for obedience. Put into action whatever you sense Holy Spirit is leading you to do. If you do not feel you get any specific instructions from Heaven, just do something good, either practical or spiritual, for someone.

As you wait on the Lord in the first half-hour, you become Spirit-filled. This is so that, in the second half-hour, you can be Spirit-spilled into the lives of others. By doing such things you will make God to be real in both your own life and in the lives of the people you touch.

Give Holy Spirit an hour of your life per week more than you are doing now. The first half-hour is for you to receive and be Spirit-filled. The second half-hour is to do something for someone, so that you can be Spirit-spilled in Kingdom ministry

My final point is this:

> *¹⁷ Therefore do not be vague and thoughtless and foolish, but understanding and firmly grasping what the will of the Lord is. ¹⁸ And do not get drunk with wine, for that is debauchery [wild living – ISV; reckless actions – Holman Study Bible]; but ever be filled and stimulated with the [Holy] Spirit.*
> *Ephesians 5:17-18 AMP*

The International Standard Version ends verse 18 like this: "keep on being filled with the Spirit."

When I was first saved, lots of years ago, we were taught the following saying; It is founded on New Testament truth, including Ephesians 5:18 and the testimony of Peter in Acts 2:4, Acts 4:8 and Acts 4:31: "One baptism in Holy Spirit, many infillings."

So, please make it a priority to be filled with Holy Spirit and stay filled with Him, because we are needed to be His instruments in this world.

Lessons From My Dog

Unfortunately, life and ministry can both deplete us. We need to intentionally stay Spirit-filled and to always be thirsty for more of God in our lives, as well as desiring more from God.

What is one thing you have learned from this teaching?

What is one thing you can do to implement this teaching?

Faith Declaration:

I thank You Lord for giving me your Holy Spirit as my Helper. Forgive me Lord for times when I have grieved Him, resisted Him, neglected Him, disobeyed Him or quenched Him. I praise You for the empowering Holy Spirit brings into my life, so that I am more like Christ in my character, behaviour and ministry. I am thirsty for more of You God and more from You Lord, by Your Holy Spirit. Right now I stir up my faith to hear You, to be filled with You and to be used by You. I say here I am Lord, fill me, send me, use me for Your glory and people's benefit, in Jesus' Name. Lord by faith I declare I am ready for both the natural and supernatural things You have in store for me and for others through me. I look not to my feelings, but to You Lord and to Your Word. I declare in Jesus' Name that as I step out in love and faith, Holy Spirit will be activated to do the works God wants done. Amen

29 Holy Spirit, our Standby:
From Atmosphere to Action

However, I am telling you nothing but the truth when I say it is profitable (good, expedient, advantageous) for you that I go away. Because if I do not go away, the Comforter (Counsellor, Helper, Advocate, Intercessor, Strengthener, Standby) will not come to you [into close fellowship with you]; but if I go away, I will send Him to you [to be in close fellowship with you].

John 16:7 AMP.

(i) The Advantage of having Holy Spirit in your life

Surely this must have seemed to be the most ridiculous and unwelcome statement Jesus ever made to his closest friends and disciples. It was equalled in its unwelcome-ness by Jesus' predictions of His suffering and death. However, while these passion and triumph prophecies were mysterious, they were definitely not ridiculous.

Put yourself in their place. Would you rather have the visible, personal, wise, miracle-working Jesus with you, or have Him send along someone that you might assume would be like a substitute teacher at school, when your real teacher is away due to sickness?

Another way of putting yourself in their mind-set is to imagine Jesus being like your closest companion, who is a mixture of Bill Gates the richest man in the world, Einstein possibly the smartest man who ever lived and Arnold Schwarzenegger (or whoever was the strongest man in the world).

Whenever you were confronted with an opportunity or a challenge, you could ask Bill to pay for it or Einstein to figure it out or Arnie to break through the obstacle with brute force. That's what it was like for them to have Jesus with them. Can you see how hard it would have been for the disciples to understand how Jesus' departure would be in any way advantageous to them?

What they didn't realise was that they would be scattered to lots of nations and places. Because Jesus was limited to being in a physical body, He could only be in one place at any one time. When the omnipresent, omniscient, omnipotent Holy Spirit came to live inside them, He would be with them and all believers wherever they were anywhere and everywhere in the world, all the time. What an advantage that is.

Jesus gave them, and us, a clue about this Paraclete Who was to come, when He used the clarifying adjective "allos" (in the Greek) to say "another" Helper. (John 14:16 NAS). This Greek word indicates that Jesus was saying the Holy Spirit would be another Helper of the *same kind* as Jesus Himself. In other words, Holy Spirit is a Divine Helper, Whom Christians know to be the third Person of the Trinity.

If Jesus had used the clarifying Greek word "heteros", He would have been telling them that the new helper was going to be a different kind of helper than Himself.

When we understand that Holy Spirit is just as much God as Jesus was, then His prediction makes sense. Jesus could only be in one place at a time, because He had confined Himself to a human body. Therefore, if He was in Jerusalem and He sent the disciples to Galilee, He could not be with them.

On the other hand, because Holy Spirit is as omni-present as God, He can be with each and every disciple in equal measure all the time, even if they are scattered throughout every nation on the face of the earth.

Now that is a great advantage for every believer to have in life and ministry, just as Jesus said – isn't it?

> **New Testament Christians have the advantage of the Divine, Omniscient, Omnipotent, Omnipresent Holy Spirit with each and every one of us, all the time, everywhere. This is better than having Bill Gates, Einstein and Arnold Schwarzenegger as our companions.**

(ii) 7 Holy Spirit descriptions in John 16:7 AMP

I love the seven words the Amplified Bible uses to describe Holy Spirit. Of course, He is many other things as well, including our teacher, our guide, the One Who convicts us of sin, righteousness and judgement to come and sanctifies us, and Who empowers us to grow the fruit of the Spirit and to minister to others using His supernatural, spiritual gifts.

Let me remind you of just one thing concerning each of these seven descriptive names of Holy Spirit.

(a) Comforter

When you are in pain or mourning, He is there with you as your Comforter. You may not feel the actual touch of the arms of God around you, but you can be sure they are there, because He is there. (Deuteronomy 33:27). He will ease your inner pain, fill you with God's love and sustain you with His power until you are at peace again.

(b) Counsellor

When you are confused about what to decide or do, Holy Spirit is there as your Counsellor, to impart God's wisdom to you, either directly or through someone who helps you make the right decision. (James 1:5-7). He also counsels you through the Bible that He wrote through many people.

(c) Helper

When you need a friend, a partner to get you through a tough situation or to take advantage of a great opportunity, Holy Spirit is your Helper. He can enable you to do what you cannot do on your own. He can give you favour with important people. He can arrange the release of the resources you need to succeed. (Ecclesiastes 4:9-12).

(d) Advocate

As your Advocate, Holy Spirit speaks to the Father on your behalf. He counters the devil's accusations against you, because you have been forgiven of your sins. He also works on your behalf when your reputation is attacked, both to give you peace and self-control and to work for your righteousness to be affirmed. (Psalm 103:6 NLT).

(e) Intercessor

Prayer is the most important source of power in the universe. Prayer is our God-given means of building both personal relationship and partnership with the All-Mighty. Prayer is not one-sided. We talk to God and He talks to us. As our Intercessor, Holy Spirit prays to the Father for us, just as Jesus told Peter that He had prayed for them. (Luke 22:31-32). He also inspires our praying, so that we get Divine results. I must also gladly tell you that Holy Spirit's intercession will always lead to Holy Spirit's active intervention on your behalf. Hallelujah.

Holy Spirit's intercession, either direct to God on your behalf or through you in inspired prayer, will always lead to Holy Spirit's active intervention on your behalf.

(f) Strengthener

We all have times when we feel weak. This is when we must call upon Holy Spirit to be our Strengthener. Having done so, we must act in faith as if He had answered our prayer. Joel 3:10b says: *"…. let the weak say I am strong!"* So, you must stop confessing your weakness and declare that you are strong in the Lord and in the power of His might. Then you will act as if you were strong.

By faith, you do what you think a strong person, a strong Christian, a strong believer would do in your situation. If you need to get someone else to help you be strong and act strong, then enlist their help and just do it.

(g) Standby

The key to experiencing all the things promised by the other six Holy Spirit Names is found in the final descriptive "Standby". When you get home from work or shopping or play and the television is turned off, but plugged in to the power supply, what colour is the power light? Here in Australia, it is mostly red. This signifies that the television is on standby.

What do you have to do to watch a program? Of course, you have to press the power button on your remote. What happens to the light? It turns to green. What happens to the black television screen? It comes alive with beautiful colours and simultaneously sound fills the room.

Holy Spirit as Standby is like that. He is waiting for you to switch Him into action mode. How? In chapter 2 of my book, *"You Can Prophesy – Supernatural. Simple. Safe."*, I wrote about the normal kinds of Christian activities that spark Holy Spirit into action. I mentioned:

- Prayer
- Praise and Worship
- Repentance, Righteousness and Obedience
- Faith
- Financial Giving

- Unity
- Honour
- Evangelism

Let me challenge you to stir up Holy Spirit Partnership and ministry in and through your life. He does not want to be your silent partner. He does not want to be your junior partner.

Holy Spirit does not want to be your silent partner, nor your junior partner. By faith, you must activate Him from Standby mode to active, Divine function.

God has work to do in this earth. It's up to you to surrender to Him and put your faith into action. Then, Holy Spirit will do far more good and great things for you and through you. You will be blessed, because you are being a blessing to both God and man. People will be encouraged, touched and transformed. The Lord will be glorified. How good is that! So, Go For It!

What is one thing you have learned from this teaching?

What is one thing you can do to implement this teaching?

Faith Declaration:

I thank You, Holy Spirit, that it is to my advantage to have You in my life. I thank You for being my Comforter Counsellor, Helper, Advocate, Intercessor, Strengthener and Standby. I switch You into active partnership mode, by my love and faith and obedience right now. I expect Your manifest Presence in me, with me, around me and through me to others this day and every day, in Jesus' mighty Name. Amen. I confess that You and I will turn every positive opportunity into a successful outcome and every negative situation into a victory for the glory of God.

30   Healing *and* Salvation

Surely our griefs (or "sickness") He Himself bore, and our sorrows (or "pains") He carried. Yet we ourselves esteemed Him stricken, Smitten of God, and afflicted. ⁵ But He was pierced through (or "wounded") for our transgressions, He was crushed for our iniquities; the chastening for our well-being (or "peace") fell upon Him, and by His scourging we are healed.

Isaiah 53:4-5 NAS

I want to share with you why I believe salvation includes physical healing. This is important, because if Jesus died for both our sickness and our sins, then by faith we can receive healing and freedom from our symptoms (because the causes thereof are healed), just as by faith we receive forgiveness and freedom from guilt, shame and condemnation.

(1)   The Broad Meaning of "Salvation" includes Physical Healing

My first reason for believing that physical healing is included in the atonement suffering, sacrifice and triumph of Jesus has to do with the meaning of the word "salvation".

The very Name "Jesus" means "God saves". So, included in His Name is a statement of what Jesus came to earth to do. It wasn't just to buy believers a spiritual bus ticket to heaven or an escape pass from hell when they die.

Lessons From My Dog

The most prominent Hebrew word for salvation in the Old Testament is "yasa". In the New Testament the Greek words "sozo" (verb) or "soteria" (noun) are used. The way these words are used indicate that salvation is not restricted to the spiritual dimension, meaning salvation from the penalty and power of sin. Salvation also encompasses the material, circumstantial, psychological and physiological.

The Name "Jesus", which is the Greek equivalent of the Hebrew "Joshua", means "God saves" or "God is salvation". The emphasis of the New Testament is on Jesus saving lost people from sin. (Matthew 1:21-23; Luke 19:10). However, in the Gospels, Holy Spirit through the inspired writers, uses the broader meaning of salvation to specifically and explicitly include physical healing.

For example in Mark 6:56, whoever was physically sick and touched the hem of Jesus' garment, just like the woman with the issue of blood had done, was healed. The Greek word that was translated into English as "healed", in order to correctly describe what happened to the sick people, is "sozo".

This literally means that the sick were saved. They experienced a dimension of the salvation of God. The dimension they experienced was physical. They were physically saved. They were healed.

The Jews use the word "shalom", which is another multi-dimensional, whole-of-life word, as a greeting. I read once that the first Christians would greet one another, as an equivalent of the Jewish "shalom", using a derivative of "sozo", which effectively meant "how is your salvation?"

In Australia today we might ask: "How are you, my friend?" or "How're ya goin' mate?". The ancient "sozo"-based greeting, like our modern equivalent and the Jewish "shalom", was intended to ask "How is the whole of your life?"; "How is your spiritual life and your relational life and your physical life and your work life and your financial life?"

Salvation is not restricted to spiritual matters. Salvation includes physical healing and other blessings that Jesus quoted in His job description. (refer Isaiah 61:1-7; Luke 4:18-19).

On a personal level, the true and full meaning of salvation is to have wholeness of life. This occurs when you have a healthy spiritual life, which is a healthy personal relationship with our loving, holy Lord; a healthy soul (mind, will and emotions); and a healthy body. It also means having healthy relationships and healthy finances.

The Greek words translated as salvation in the New Testament, like the Hebrew word "shalom" meaning peace, are multi-dimensional, whole-of-life words. They include our spiritual life, our relational life, our physical life, our work life, our financial life and the health of our mind, will and emotions.

(ii) The Central Salvation chapter, Isaiah 53, teaches Healing in Salvation

The first is found in Isaiah's great salvation chapter.

> *⁴Surely He (Jesus) has borne ("nasa") our griefs ("choli" sicknesses, weaknesses, and distresses) and carried ("sabal") our sorrows and pains ("makob") [...], yet we [ignorantly] considered Him stricken, smitten, and afflicted by God [...]. ⁵But He was wounded for our transgressions, He was bruised for our guilt and sins; the punishment [needed to obtain] peace and well-being for us was upon Him, and with the whip-lashes [that wounded] Him we are healed and made whole. ⁶All we like sheep have gone astray, we have turned every one to his own way; and the Lord has (put) upon Him the guilt and iniquity of us all....¹¹ My righteous servant will justify many, and He will carry ("sabal") their iniquities. ¹² ... He (Jesus) bore ("nasa") [and took away] the sin of many ...*
>
> Isaiah 53:4-6, 11-12 AMP

- Verses 4 and 12 use the same Hebrew verb ("nasa"). This means that on the Cross, Jesus, our sinless, perfect, sacrificial substitute "bore" both our sins (v.12) and our "sicknesses" (the literal meaning of the Hebrew word "choli" in verse 4).

- Verses 4 and 11 use the same Hebrew verb ("sabal"). This tells us that Jesus "carried" both our iniquities (v.11) and "pains" (the literal meaning of the Hebrew word "makob" in verse 4).

By using this inter-related language, Holy Spirit is telling us in no uncertain terms that the very same acts of suffering, sacrifice and triumph by Jesus paid the price for both the forgiveness of our sins and the healing of our bodies.

Therefore, by faith, I can receive both forgiveness of and cleansing from my sins and healing of my sicknesses.

It is important to understand that the translators of the Hebrew words "choli" and "makob" in 15 out of 19 versions of the Bible used English words like griefs and sorrows, instead of their more literal meanings of illnesses and pains. I find it hard to understand why they would do this and difficult to not accuse the translators of unbelief.

It is easier for interpreters to say that Jesus heals our griefs and sorrows, rather than teach that He heals our bodies. It takes even less faith for people to interpret griefs and sorrows as being directly related to sin and referring to spiritual pain and sorrow, rather than meaning the healing of the very real and very painful physical and inner hurts people experience in life.

The translation of Matthew's reference to Isaiah 53:4-5, is a stinging indictment on the unbelief of the translators of the Hebrew.

> *When evening came, many who were demon-possessed were brought to him, and he drove out the spirits with a word and healed all the sick.*[17] *This was to fulfil what was spoken through the prophet Isaiah "He took up our infirmities and bore our diseases."*
>
> *Matthew 8:16-17*

Healing and Salvation

Holy Spirit through Matthew made this clear: He wants Bible readers to understand that Jesus paid for our physical healing and deliverance from every devilish affliction, as well as for our forgiveness and freedom from the penalty and power of sin.

Jesus carried on to the Cross both our sins and our sicknesses. Therefore, we can confidently say two things.

Firstly, that God will forgive your sins, because Jesus was punished in your place. By believing in Jesus and what He did for you, you can be spiritually saved and made ready to enter God's heaven.

Secondly, that God will heal your body, because Jesus was also punished for your pains and sicknesses to be removed from you and for you to experience His Healing Power.

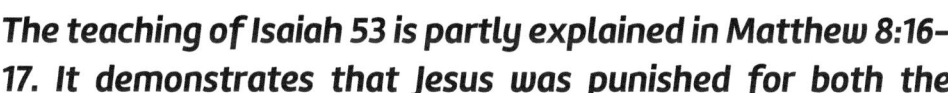

The teaching of Isaiah 53 is partly explained in Matthew 8:16-17. It demonstrates that Jesus was punished for both the forgiveness of our sins and the healing of our bodies.

Again I say: the Bible teaches that Christian salvation is not just spiritual; it is whole-of-life.

Of course it would be ridiculous to suggest that there is a Scripture which teaches the forgiveness of sins stopped when Jesus ascended to heaven. Similarly, there is no doctrine in the Bible that can change the nature of salvation. Healing of the physical body and deliverance from demonic afflictions are part and parcel of salvation. Therefore, for as long as there is salvation from sin, there is and must also be healing and deliverance.

All the promises of God in the Bible are received by grace through faith. Each and every Christian has to have his or her own faith to receive the spiritual salvation Jesus purchased for us all on the Cross. Similarly, every believer must also exercise the same personal faith in the Word of God and the work of Jesus in order to receive the physical salvation, the healing of our bodies, that our Lord has made available to us.

It is important for you, my reader, to grasp hold of this truth. So, again I say: Jesus paid for your full salvation. This means that, by faith in Jesus, spiritually you can be forgiven, cleansed, reconciled to God and become a friend of God. Also, by faith, you can experience peace of mind, a restored soul and physical healing.

In theological terms, we can say that physical healing is included in the atonement. Healing is included in the package of salvation that Jesus purchased for us by taking the punishment He did before and on the cross. He really was punished twice, firstly by flogging and then by crucifixion. I believe that double punishment was to clearly emphasise the fact that both forgiveness and healing are part of the salvation we receive by faith in the Word of God and in His undeserved and unearned grace.

(iii) "Shalom" is the gift of whole-of-life peace

In Isaiah 53:5b, we are told that the punishment Jesus took on our behalf brought us the shalom-peace of God.

Just a bit of Bible study will inform you that the Hebrew word "shalom" means much more than simply peace with God, which too many Christians think is all that is included in salvation.

Numbers 6:24-26 is a well-known priestly decree of God's shalom over the Israelites. It reads as an obviously whole-of-life blessing.

Psalm 38:4 uses the word shalom in direct relation to physical health – in that case it was in a negative context, meaning David's bones lacked the shalom-peace of God.

The prophecy of Jeremiah in chapter 33 verses 6-9 speaks of the shalom of God in an intertwined way with the concepts of healing, peace, cleansing, forgiveness and prosperity.

Shalom includes (a) peace with God; (b) peace within oneself; (c) peace in your body; (d) peace in your relationships and partnerships (e.g. 1 Kings 5:12); (e) peace in your finances and circumstances; and (f) peace and victory over adversity and opposition, which is the traditional meaning of peace in the context of war.

Shalom includes peace with God; peace within oneself; peace in your body; peace in your relationships and partnerships; (e) peace in your finances and circumstances; and peace and victory over adversity and opposition

---

When you realise the broad scope of the word "shalom", you can see that what Jesus purchased for us on the cross, by taking our punishment for us, was far more than only spiritual benefits. He also paid for our healing and wholeness in spirit, soul (mind, will and emotions) and body; our harmony with others; our victory in life and over the devil; and our provision for all we would need in this life to succeed in fulfilling the plan of God for and through our lives.

Why don't you stop right here and give Jesus and the Father thanks, because Jesus got what we deserved, which was punishment, so we could get what He deserved, which is whole-of-life blessing and provision.

(iv) The doctrine of salvation incorporating physical healing is revealed in both the Old and New Testaments

Bless the LORD, O my soul, And all that is within me, bless His holy name.² Bless the LORD, O my soul, And forget none of His benefits; ³ Who pardons all your iniquities, Who heals all your diseases;⁴ Who redeems your life from the pit, Who crowns you with lovingkindness and compassion; ⁵ Who satisfies your years with good things, So that your youth is renewed like the eagle.

Psalm 103:1-5

These verses of Psalm 103 teach us that with the same faith in the same Bible and the same God, we can experience forgiveness and healing and other benefits.

Malachi 4:2 talks about the Sun of Righteousness, Who has healing in His wings. This brings together in one Saviour the forgiveness of sin, the clothing with the holiness of Christ and the power of God to heal the sick.

> *[14] Is any one of you sick? He should call the elders of the church to pray over him and anoint him with oil in the name of the Lord. [15] And the prayer offered in faith will make the sick person well; the Lord will raise him up. If he has sinned, he will be forgiven. [16] Therefore confess your sins to each other and pray for each other so that you may be healed. The prayer of a righteous man is powerful and effective...*
>
> *James 5:14-16*

Again we see healing and forgiveness in the very same passage of Scripture. Surely the Divine pattern and Divine promise is both clear and confirmed. The Lord your God wants you to be well, as much as He wants you to be forgiven.

Jesus demonstrated this pattern when He both forgave and healed the paralysed man, who was lowered through a roof by his four friends in order to be placed before Jesus for healing. (Mark 2:1-12). Notice that Jesus saw their faith.

It is also important to note that forgiveness may be the precursor to healing, as it was in this case.

Conclusion

Anyone who believes in Jesus and in the Word of God is equally able and qualified in Christ to receive both the forgiveness of their sins and the healing of their bodies. The sacrifice of Jesus made both forgiveness and healing available to us. We do not earn, deserve or self-qualify for these blessings. God gives them freely to us in honour of His Son, Jesus. They can only be claimed by faith.

Healing and Salvation

It is important for me to emphasise that just as we cannot earn our forgiveness and our place in God's heaven, so we cannot earn our healing. The wonderful good news of the Christian Gospel is that all we need to receive God's many blessings that are freely given to us by His grace, is to have faith. We have faith in what Jesus did for each and every one of us.

No-one is more qualified or less qualified to receive healing from Jesus. He was punished so that every person of every nation and every generation could experience His full salvation for spirit, soul and body and life.

You can confidently say – and I urge you to do so out loud right now – "Healing belongs to me because of what Jesus did for me."

Many people readily accept the benefit of God's forgiveness of their sins, but fail to accept the benefit of healing for their bodies. This is partly due to the lack of preaching about healing as being included in our salvation.

Many pastors preach only part of the Gospel, the spiritual part, the "eternal life" part, which is about the forgiveness of our sins. Sadly, they ignore the natural blessings and benefits that Jesus has also made available to us – the "abundant life" aspects of salvation. The natural part of the Gospel includes healing for the mind and the body and provision for life and ministry.

For the purposes of this chapter, my key point is that whenever and wherever the "full Gospel" is preached, healing for the body is included.

I need to make my full position clear. You might ask: "Does Nick believe in doctors?" My answer is: "Yes."

I believe medical science is one aspect of the fulfilling of the prophecy in Daniel (12:4) re the "increase of knowledge". I believe the "sick need a physician" as Jesus Himself said in Mark 2:17. This is illustrated in the Old Testament by King Hezekiah's healing in Isaiah 38:21.

So, I believe in having both faith for God's Divine healing and wisdom to pursue the best medical advice and treatment that doctors can provide. However, my emphasis in this study is to say that we should go to God and His Word, not to the doctor or the pill packet, first.

I believe in having both faith for God's Divine healing and wisdom to pursue the best medical advice and treatment that doctors can provide. Doctors treat our patients, but it is God Who heals. We should go to God and His Word, not to the doctor or the pill packet, first.

The glory will always go to the Lord for our improvement and full restoration, because, as one doctor is reported to have said: We treat our patients, but it is God Who heals. This is in accord with the Bible's revelation that God gave Himself the Name "Jehovah Rapha", which means: "I am the Lord Who heals you."

The Lord has committed Himself in a covenant way to helping us get well when we are sick. Hallelujah.

Another matter I want to clarify is this: I cannot explain why some people are healed and others are not. I do not believe in blaming the patient for a lack of faith. There are many complicating and intersecting factors involved in the Divine healing of our physical conditions. I haven't got time to go into them all here.

My goal in this chapter is to inspire you to believe God for Divine healing and not be limited to medical science, nor to a "che sera sera" approach, which fatalistically represents thinking that "whatever will be, will be."

Healing and Salvation

What is one thing you have learned from this teaching?

What is one thing you can do to implement this teaching?

Faith Declaration:

I thank You Lord that you have made available to me so many benefits in the Gospel and by the suffering, sacrifice and triumph of Your Divine Son Jesus, my Saviour, Healer, Provider and Lord. I praise You because I can confidently say: Healing belongs to me because of what Jesus did for me. Right now in Jesus' Name, I claim my healings and I command my body to come into line with the Word of God, and to serve the Lord and His purpose by serving me in fullness of bodily health and strength, in Jesus' Name. Amen

31 Faith Confessions
Make a Difference

⁷ So I prophesied as I was commanded. And as I was prophesying, there was a noise, a rattling sound, and the bones came together, bone to bone. ⁸ I looked, and tendons and flesh appeared on them and skin covered them, but there was no breath in them. ⁹ Then (the Lord) said to me, "Prophesy to the breath; prophesy, son of man, and say to it, 'This is what the Sovereign LORD says: Come, breath, from the four winds and breathe into these slain, that they may live.'" ¹⁰ So I prophesied as He commanded me, and breath entered them; they came to life and stood up on their feet — a vast army.

Ezekiel 37:7-10

(i) Are you positive or negative enough to start speaking the Word of God over your life?

If you have heard the testimony of Reinhard Bonnke, you will know that his miracle ministry began because the Lord said to him: "My Words in your mouth are as powerful as My words in My mouth."

A stunning example of what the Lord said to Bonnke in action is found in the famous passage of the valley of dry bones in Ezekiel 37:1-10. As the prophet spoke what God told him to prophesy, miracle working power was released, sufficient to bring the defeated, disunited, dry, dead army to life as an effective fighting force that could liberate captives and possess inheritances wherever they went.

Faith Confessions Make a Difference

Twice in this passage the prophet says that he spoke the words God told him. Each time, his words of faith triggered the manifestation of the very miracles that God wanted to happen.

Understand that these bones were well and truly beyond all human repair. Only God could change their condition. They stayed defeated, dry, dead and disconnected until the prophet spoke the Word of God over them. Then they were raised up as a great and mighty army.

- How defeated, dry, dead or disconnected do you feel?
- Are you defeated, dry, dead or disconnected enough to do something about your situation?
- Are you defeated, dry, dead or disconnected enough to do something that God has ordained about your situation?
- Are you defeated, dry, dead or disconnected enough to put God's Word into action, by praising Him always and anyway, and by speaking the relevant Scriptures in His Word over your particular situation and circumstances?

The miracle in the valley of dry bones demonstrates that Divine power is released by a Christian's verbal decree of God's Word over even impossible situations and circumstances. When you speak God's Word in faith, you will activate the miracle-working power of the Holy Spirit into your situation.

Job 22:28 explains the power of decree

Job provides another Old Testament example of this Divine principle by which words spoken in faith result in the manifestation of the things spoken. Again, I stress that Christians should speak the Word of God over their lives, families, circumstances and futures.

There is not time in this chapter to consider the powerful passage of Job 22:21-29, but I urge you to read it.

> *You shall also decide and decree a thing, and it shall be established for you; and the light [of God's favour] shall shine upon your ways.*
>
> *Job 22:28 AMP*

The Hebrew word here translated "established" literally means to "arise, stand up". In other words, what you speak over yourself and your situation will become a reality in your life.

Job 22:28 says that you shall decide and decree a thing and, by God's grace and power, it shall arise and become a reality in your life.

Job 22:28 says, in effect: you say it and God will do it. This is a key verse in understanding the power of decree.

> *You'll take delight in God, the Mighty One, and look to Him joyfully, boldly. You'll pray to Him and He'll listen; He'll help you do what you've promised. You'll decide what you want and it will happen; your life will be bathed in light.*
>
> *Job 22:26-28 T.M.*

The NIV translates the first part of verse 28 as: "What you decide on will be done;" The NLT version is: "You will succeed in whatever you choose to do."

These alternative versions emphasise the fact that God will bless what you choose to decree. Of course, the broader principle of the Word of God is that we don't speak just anything that pops into our head. We decree what God says and what God wills.

Holy Spirit through the psalmist expressed the same principle in the specific ministry of healing.

He sent His word and healed them.
Psalm 107:20

(iii) 2 Corinthians 1:20 says it best in the New Testament

Let's look at the New Testament. Here are three different versions of 2 Corinthians 1:20

For no matter how many promises God has made, they are "Yes" in Christ. And so through Him the "Amen" is spoken by us to the glory of God.
2 Corinthians 1:20 NIV

For all the promises of God find their Yes in him. That is why it is through Him that we utter our Amen to God for His glory.
2 Corinthians 1:20 ESV

For all the promises of God, whatever their number, have their confirmation in Him; and for this reason through Him also our "Amen" acknowledges their truth and promotes the glory of God through our faith.
2 Corinthians 1:20 Weymouth

Here's the key point of this verse:

Jesus has said "Yes" to and made all the promises of God in the Bible available to us; but we must say the "Amen." Our words of faith are required in order for those promises to become a reality in our lives.

Jesus said "Yes" to all the promises of God, thereby making them all available to us. We must say the "Amen" in active faith, by words and actions, in order to make those promises a reality in our lives

---

(iv) The choice is yours – don't blame God

If people choose to not activate this Divine miracle-working method, to not speak in agreement with God's Word, then the promises of God will probably remain just a spiritual theory on the pages of the Bible for them.

Sadly, many uncooperative, unbelieving Christians will remain frustrated and be deceived into thinking that God does not love them or His Word does not work for them.

Let me be clear: if Christians choose to not obey, or to not speak in agreement with God's Word, then there is no guarantee that the covenant promises of God will become real in their lives simply by the Lord deciding to drop blessings and miracles into their laps, regardless of their refusal to co-operate with Him or their lack of faith in His Word. (Hebrews 3:18–4:2).

Some time ago Holy Spirit revealed this to me: when you do what the Bible says, God will do what the Bible says. Putting this revelation in the context of this chapter, it means: When by faith you say what the Bible says, God will do what the Bible says. Amen to that!

When you speak God's Words in faith, you release Holy Spirit to do good things and those good things start to happen.

(v) Persistence pays good dividends

Warning: This is a lifestyle issue of faith, not a matter of trying it once to see if it works. I have said before that persistence overcomes enemy resistance. I need also to say, as illustrated in Jesus' parables of the unjust judge (Luke 18:1-8) and the friend who came for bread at midnight (Luke 11:5-8), you must persist in faith in order to see your miracle manifest.

God is not reluctant to bless us. Indeed He has "much more" that He wants to give us. We need to persist in order to prove the genuineness of our faith, the reality of our trust in Him and our determination to receive our miracle. Consider those who pushed through in faith to get their miracles, including the woman with the issue of blood (Luke 8:43-48), the Syrophonecian mother (Matthew 15:21-28) and the four friends who broke a hole in someone's roof in order to get a miracle from Jesus for their paralysed buddy. (Mark 2:1-12).

Persisting in faith pays miraculous dividends

Christians must know what the Bible says, believe what the Bible says and say what the Bible says!

By faith, let the weak, say "I am strong." (Joel 3:10).

By faith, let the intimidated Gideon, say: "I am a mighty man of valour." (Judges 6:12).

By faith, let the childless Abraham, say: "I am a father of many nations." (Genesis 17:5).

By faith, let those who fear they cannot, say: "I can do all things through Christ Who strengthens me." (Philippians 4:13). Note: Don't say "I can't", when God says "you can".

Another reason for persisting in faith with the confession of God's word is found in Romans 10:17. As you speak the Word of God, your own faith will grow, so that you can believe for the manifestation of the promises of God. As your faith grows, you will not let the devil, or people or life's circumstances, life's seasons or life's disappointments rob you of your blessings or miracles.

You will start to believe again that:

- your life will be better
- your marriage will improve,
- your children will return to the Lord
- your finances will increase and your debts decrease,
- your body will be healed,

- your mind will be at peace,
- your emotions will experience the joy of the Lord,
- your mourning will be turned to dancing,
- your spiritual enemies will retreat
- the defeat they were trying to impose upon you will become a victory for the glory of the Lord
- your ministry will be abundantly blessed.

Of course the devil will fight you all the way to rob you of your inheritance in every area of life. Praise God, there is a way to defeat him and be blessed despite his impeding efforts.

They triumphed over him (the devil) by Blood of the Lamb and by the word of their testimony;
Revelation 12:11

These believers spoke the words of the Bible and their own stories of God's partnership in and favour over their lives. When they did this, the devil retreated from them, just as he did when Jesus resisted him with the word of God, when He was tempted in the wilderness. (Luke 4:1-13).

Why do spoken words help defeat the devil? Because God has ordained it to be so. Remember the words have to be spoken in faith, and be in agreement with God's Word.

Faith Confessions Make a Difference

What is one thing you have learned from this teaching?

What is one thing you can do to implement this teaching?

Faith Declarations:

- In Christ, I have been delegated Divine authority (Luke 10:19; Matthew 28:18-20). In Jesus' Name, I speak Divine protection and provision into being over myself, my family and my church family, each and all. (Psalms 91 and 121; John 10:10).

- I will not fear what man or life or the devil do to me, because The Lord is on my side and no weapon formed against me shall prosper. (Psalm 118:6-7; Isaiah 54:17)

- In Jesus' name, I speak God's Peace over my life and family. I declare Peace in my mind; in my emotions; in my body; in my family and in all my relationships and partnerships. (Isaiah 53:4,5)

- I thank You Father God that Your mercies are new every morning. (Lamentations 3:21-25). I thank You Lord that today I will not be dominated by any of the negatives of my distant or recent past. In Jesus' Name, I receive Your forgiveness and give it to people who have hurt or offended me. I also receive my healing and freedom from every such thing. I bless my new day and my future in Jesus' Name with the blessings of Heaven above and of the earth, because I have All-Mighty God as my Divine Helper. (Ephesians 1:3; Genesis 49:22,25,26).

32 Journey to Double Portion: *Gilgal*

When the Lord was about to take Elijah up to heaven in a whirlwind, Elijah and Elisha were on their way from Gilgal.² Elijah said to Elisha, "Stay here; the Lord has sent me to Bethel." But Elisha said, "As surely as the Lord lives and as you live, I will not leave you"

⁹ When they had crossed, Elijah said to Elisha, "Tell me, what can I do for you before I am taken from you?" "Let me inherit a double portion of your spirit," Elisha replied.

2 Kings 2:1–2 and 9

The journey Elisha took to inherit the double portion has much to tell us today about how we can position ourselves to receive a double portion anointing from God. In Elisha's case it was for ministry. For us, it may be for ministry or business or family or any area of our life. The Lord wants to equip and resource His people to succeed in all seven significant areas of society, namely: family, church, government, education, business, media and art/sport/entertainment.

There were four places the two prophets visited on this journey. Of course, the refusal of Elisha to stop at any of those places as Elijah instructed him to is a lesson in itself. It's not about disobeying our overseers, because both prophets knew the instruction was not for obedience but to test Elisha's persistence in pursuing Elijah's mantle.

We will not reach our full potential in God without persistence that is fuelled by a hunger for more of Him and more from Him.

The four places Elijah and Elisha visited have some great lessons for us, regarding how to position ourselves for greater things in God. Let's look at what happened when Israel came to Gilgal.

(i)   Circumcision

Gilgal was the place where every man in Israel was circumcised and where they celebrated the Passover for the first time in a generation. These two things are symbolic of being born again. Of course, no one can be anointed, much less receive a double portion, without first becoming a born again child of God, through repentance and faith in Jesus Christ.

But let me mention some things that are more subtle and yet very significant about the circumcision at Gilgal:

Romans 2:25-29 tells us that the primary symbolism of physical circumcision is to represent the circumcision of the heart. This means a cutting away of the old, worldly way of life fuelled by the sin-loving Adamic nature. Instead, we live in a Christ-like way, empowered by Holy Spirit, demonstrating holiness of life in thoughts, words and actions.

Let me ask you to think about this question: Why did God choose that sign of the Covenant?

Why did the Lord not choose a tattoo, whether hidden or public? Leviticus 19:28 rules out that option.

Why not the famous American Indian wrist-scarring? That is ruled out by the fact that the only human blood God ordained to be shed was that of His Own Son, our Lord Jesus Christ, who suffered, sacrificed His life and rose triumphantly again for our salvation.

What about the love-slave symbol of ear-piercing? (Exodus 21:2-6). Paul calls himself the New Testament equivalent of this in Romans 1 verse 1. The Lord in His infinite wisdom chose a covenant sign that was far richer in meaning than this.

Now I am not going to describe male circumcision here, but I will explain the symbolism I believe underlies God's choice of this particular covenant sign.

(a) Circumcision indicates how very personal our relationship with God is and that there is nothing in our lives which is too private for God. Let's face it, God is omniscient. (Hebrews 4:13). There is nothing that is hid from His sight anyway, so why bother trying, the way Adam and Eve did? It didn't work for them. It won't work for us.

(b) Circumcision represents giving our sexuality to God. This means that Christ-followers choose to live sexually according to the boundaries in the Word of God, which exclude sex outside of marriage and homosexuality.

(c) Circumcision signifies that our productivity and creativity depend on God.

Circumcision represents (a) not trying to hide anything from our all-seeing, all-knowing God; (b) living in sexual purity and obedience to God's Word; (c) trusting God for and partnering with Him in areas of the creativity and productivity of our lives and ministries.

(ii) Protection in times of vulnerability

Gilgal also testifies that God will protect us in our times of vulnerability. Perhaps you know how distracting an unattended splinter in your finger can be. Imagine what a couple of stones in your shoes would feel like. Now multiply those by a hundred or a thousand and you might have an idea of how the Jewish army was feeling after their un-anaesthetised circumcisions. Those soldiers were incapable of fighting or resisting their enemy. If the Jericho under-12 girls arm-wrestling team had come out against them, the girls would have won easily.

The Lord protected them in their time of vulnerability. He has promised to do the same for you and me.

> *Even when I walk through the darkest valley, I will not be afraid, for you are close beside me. Your rod and your staff protect and comfort me.*
> Psalm 23:4 NLT

When I have been stretched to my limit physically, emotionally or spiritually, I have asked the Lord to keep any further attacks or pressure from the enemy from me until I was replenished. You can do that too. God will protect, sustain, heal and re-energise you.

> *No temptation has overtaken you except what is common to mankind. And God is faithful; He will not let you be tempted beyond what you can bear. But when you are tempted, He will also provide a way out so that you can endure it.*
> 1 Corinthians 10:13

(iii)   Inner healing and renewing the mind

Gilgal literally means "rolling". The site was named this because of what the Lord said.

> *Today I have rolled away the reproach of Egypt from you.*
> Joshua 5:9

In other words, as they submitted to physical circumcision, God did some internal miracles for them. Their circumcision at Gilgal also represents the healing of their souls and the renewing of their minds.

The Lord removed the stigma of their slavery in Egypt from them. The Hebrew word translated "reproach" in that verse is "cherpah", which also means "shame; disgrace; contempt; scorn".

Lessons From My Dog

Firstly, God removed from them and healed them of their feelings of inferiority and shame. They had a 400-year history, which is at least five generations of poverty and slavery and abuse.

What mind-set would you have about yourself if you were in the position where you could say: "I am a sanitary worker, my dad was a sanitary worker, his dad was a sanitary worker, and so on?" With apologies to those in this field of work, can you imagine what it must do to a person's thinking about their potential and future if their family history, perhaps going back to their great-great-grandfather and beyond even that, was the same lowly position?

Praise God, you can break out of that and break into your true Divine potential and destiny. The founders of the movement I have served my whole Christian life, the Apostolic Church of Australia, which was birthed by pioneers from the Apostolic Churches of Wales, Scotland and England, did. Those founding leaders were Welsh miners, whose fathers were Welsh miners, whose fathers were Welsh miners etc. They rose up under the calling and anointing of the Lord to be mighty apostolic, miracle-working church planters and builders whose influence has circled the globe. They were led by the Spirit with supernatural prophetic revelation. They had passion for God, for His Word and for people everywhere. The miracle-working power of the Lord was evident in their ministries. In Australia they filled every town hall in every capital city. This was unprecedented. Some of the miracles God did were literally front page news.

God had to break similar, but worse, negative mind-sets off Israel before they could step into their new and true destiny.

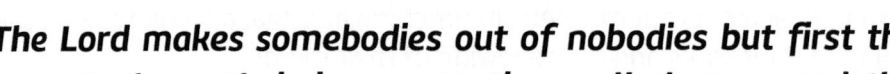

The Lord makes somebodies out of nobodies but first they have to have their inner negatives rolled away and their mind-sets changed.

Simultaneously, the Lord also eradicated the emotional bondage of the scornful put-downs of the Egyptians.

You too must, with the Lord's help, step away from and step out of the grip of your negative past, including both bad experiences and bad words spoken over you, and step into the mercies, blessings and power of God that are new every morning.

Don't let your past rob you of your future destiny. No one can experience a double portion if they think they are a good-for-nothing, poor, inferior person, or if they are paralysed by fear, as the Jewish army was when Goliath taunted them. Through the words of the Bible, God says we are His chosen sons and daughters, His powerful people, His ambassadors, who represent and re-present Christ on earth.

No one can experience a double portion if they think they are a good-for-nothing, poor, inferior person, or if they are paralysed by fear

---

(iv) Promised Land benefits and battles

There is another significant thing that happened at Gilgal. The daily manna stopped; but the Bible says *"that year they ate the produce of Canaan"*. (Joshua 5:12).

Like Israel, you must choose one of three alternative lifestyles, namely, (a) slavery in Egypt, which represents people who are not yet saved and are still slaves to sin; (b) a Christian life of wandering in the wilderness; or (c) taking your promised land, your inheritance in Christ and fulfilling your divine potential and God-given purpose in life. Each option has a price tag and a set of consequences.

(a) Slaves are in bondage and have a victim mentality. If they are lucky, they have a roof over their head and enough food and water to survive. But their workload is far more than it should be and they may often be punished, even if they don't deserve it, and possibly far more severely than their mistake warranted. No-one would want to be a slave and certainly not the devil's slave, because he is the hardest and worst slave-master of them all.

Sadly, some people in the world today can't get out of literal slavery. Others are in terrible circumstances of life and they cannot see a way out, emotionally, financially or physically. They are too scared to ask for help. They feel they have nowhere else to go. We Christians need to pray for such people and help the ones we can.

(b) Wilderness people simply survive and go nowhere with their life. They are glad to be free, but stuck in a lifestyle of just getting by spiritually and in other ways. Their faith is not well developed enough to reap the benefits of the new covenant Jesus initiated and fulfilled all the conditions for on the Cross.

Their life is just a cycle of going round and round the same mulberry bush or up and down the same mountain, year after year, like people who grow old without ever growing up. They have no real purpose, vision, dream or goals that motivate them to get up every morning. They do not have the personal relationship with God that puts them in the centre of His will for their lives. They do not have the personal partnership with the Lord that empowers them to maximize who they are and what their impact is on their world and generation. They exemplify mediocrity of Christian thinking and living.

(c) Promised Land Christians do not have the best of everything just drop into their lap. They must fight the good fight of faith for their prosperity and freedom. For Israel, as they came into Canaan, the manna stopped and the fighting began in earnest.

Jesus Himself said we will not enter into the abundant life He came to give us without having to confront the devil for it. Jesus said the devil would do everything in his power to stop us inheriting the best that God has for us. (John 10:10).

Promised Land Christians are committed to advancing the Kingdom of God on earth, in all seven spheres of society, namely, Family, Church, Government, Education, Business, Media and Art-Sport-Entertainment.

If you want to be a Promised Land Christian, you will need to use your faith and every spiritual weapon the Lord has made available to you.

You cannot be a double portion Christian if you think God is just going to drop more blessings and resources into your lap. You have to go out and use what you already have to possess your promised land. When you use what you have, God will give you more. That's the principle of sowing and reaping. God will always give you a harvest greater than what you sow.

(v) Now is the time to start or start again

> .... And who knows but that you have come to your royal position for such a time as this?"
> Esther 4:14

> For He says, "In the time of My favour I heard you, and in the day of salvation I" I tell you, now is the time of God's favour, now is the day of salvation.
> 2 Corinthians 6:2

There is another lesson of note that we can learn from Gilgal. They had not observed Circumcision or Passover for almost 40 years.

It doesn't matter if you have neglected God or been disobedient to Him in the past, what counts is what you do now, this year and for the rest of your life. Get on board with God and His purpose for your life, either for the first time or again, starting right now.

God is faithful and merciful. He knows how we are formed, He remembers that we are dust. (Psalm 103:14). He is the God of the second chance and the twenty second chance and the two thousand and second chance. But be aware even God's patience does have limits, so don't put Him to the test.

You need to get your spiritual act together. You need to get your relationship and partnership with God in correct order and function. Holy Spirit will help you do these things. When you do this consistently, you will become a promised land Christian. Then, in the words of Isaiah (1:19 and 55:2), you will enjoy what is good and delight in the richest of both heavenly and earthly blessings and provisions from the Lord.

What is one thing you have learned from this teaching?

_____

What is one thing you can do to implement this teaching?

_____

Faith Declaration:

I thank You Lord for giving me new life within and without. I am so grateful that You have rolled away all the negativity of my past life. I am grateful for Your Holy Spirit helping me live pleasing unto You and in close relationship and partnership with You. I praise You for calling me and empowering me to think and live and act like a promised land Christian. I thank You for every victory in my life, past, present and future. Lord I dedicate myself completely, in a fresh way, to You today. I commit myself to walking with You and for You by faith. I look forward to receiving my full inheritance in Christ here on earth and in Heaven for all eternity and I declare it will be so, in Jesus' Mighty Name. Amen.

33 Journey to Double Portion:
Bethel, Jericho and Jordan

> ² Elijah said to Elisha, "Stay here; the LORD has sent me to Bethel." But Elisha said, "As surely as the LORD lives and as you live, I will not leave you." So they went down to Bethel. ...⁹ When they had crossed, Elijah said to Elisha, "Tell me, what can I do for you before I am taken from you?" "Let me inherit a double portion of your spirit," Elisha replied.
>
> 2 Kings 2:2 and 9

In this chapter, we continue to walk with the two prophets Elijah and Elisha on the way to receiving our double portion using the same spiritual principles as Elisha did.

They started at Gilgal and went to three other places, which also have spiritual significance and lessons for us.

(i) Bethel, the House of God

The second place the two prophets went to on this double portion journey was Bethel, which literally means "the House of God". This was the place where Jacob dreamed of angels ascending and descending on God's Stairway to Heaven. In his prophetic dream, Jacob saw the Lord, Who made a covenant of protection and prosperity with him. (Genesis 28:12-15).

(a)   Bethel teaches us about our response to the Presence and Partnership of God

This Divine encounter and Divine promise gave Jacob real confidence about his future, so much so that he immediately committed himself to a lifestyle of financial tithing. It's important to note that this giving was voluntary on Jacob's part. It was a gift of gratitude, not fulfilling a law. Jacob willingly, cheerfully and heartfully chose to give to God a tenth of his income and increase, as a lifestyle. (Genesis 28:21). This is how the apostle Paul was told by Holy Spirit to describe godly giving in 2 Corinthians 9:8.

Financial giving to God is a heart matter. I wrote about this in my first book "*You Can Prophesy – Supernatural. Simple. Safe.*"

In Malachi 3:7 The Lord says His people have strayed from relationship with Him. The result is that He has withdrawn His Presence from them. The absence of the Presence of God has resulted in them being under a curse and suffering losses from various crop-destroying pests and diseases. They were in a very similar position to that described in Haggai 1:5,6,9-11 and 2:15-19.

In this passage in Malachi the Lord indicates that he misses and covets their company. He wants to be with His people. So, He tells them how this can happen.

Of course, we all know how to get closer to the Lord. We can read our Bible more. We can pray, praise and worship more. We can go to church and connect groups more. Maybe we can serve and witness more. We can examine our heart and lifestyle to see if we have any sin problems.

God says in verse 7 that obedience or disobedience in regard to tithing is a relationship issue.

Now, consider what Jesus taught in John 14:21 and 23. Those who love God, obey Him … and they are rewarded with His presence. So a Christian's disobedience is a love issue, a relationship issue.

That's why the Lord says in Malachi, if you want to return to Me in relationship, then show Me you love Me by obeying My principle of tithing.

Lessons From My Dog

I have a number of favourite sayings. The following one is so good that it deserves to be in the Bible. I believe it encapsulates what God is saying in these verses.

"You can give without loving" (say, by paying your taxes, electricity bills and credit card debts); "but you cannot love without giving."

Here's the principle that is revealed in this passage from Malachi 3: If you have a problem with giving to God, then you have a problem with loving God.

Financial giving to God is a relationship issue. If you have a problem with giving to God, then you have a problem with loving God. You can give without loving, but you cannot love without giving.

If you are a son of God, you will have real confidence about your future and you will be unafraid to live by faith. This is because you know God, His Nature and His Word. He is a rewarder of those who love Him, believe in Him and obey Him. (Hebrews 11:6).

In the area of your finances, and in every other area of life, you can't expect God's reward, nor His double portion, if you haven't got the faith to live your life financially God's way.

If we want to receive the double portion, we've got to believe for it and then put our faith into action ... as a lifestyle.

(b) Bethel reminds us that God is faithful to His promises and will do far, far more for us His children, than we could ever ask or think. (Matthew 7:11; Ephesians 3:20).

(c) Bethel also represents a desire to know God, a hunger to be in His presence and a commitment to the house of God.

It's not good enough to want God's blessing or power, we must want Him. Don't seek only the gift, seek the Giver. Don't seek only the healing, seek the Healer.

> *One thing have I desired of the LORD, that will I seek after – that I may dwell in the house of the LORD all the days of my life, to behold the beauty of the LORD, and to enquire in His temple.*
>
> *Psalm 27:4*

We can ask God for many things, all the promises of God in fact, but what really matters to the Lord is, do we want God Himself? Or, do we only want what God can do for us?

Do we love God with all our heart and soul and mind and strength? Or, do we just love His blessing?

(d) Bethel, the House of God, reminds us of the importance of being active and consistent members of your local church.

I want you to notice that twice in this verse (Psalm 27:4) the togetherness aspect of Christianity is emphasised. The Psalmist mentions the house and the temple of the Lord, the place of the gathering together of the people of God.

So let me ask you this question: How much of a priority is church in your life? Can people see that you seek first the Kingdom of God, because you are a regular church-goer?

> *Let us consider and give attentive, watching over one another, studying how we may stir up (stimulate and incite) to love and helpful deeds and noble activities, [25] not forsaking or neglecting to assemble together [as believers], as is the habit of some people, but admonishing (warning, urging, and encouraging) one another, and all the more faithfully as you see the day (of our Lord's return) approaching.*
>
> *Hebrews 10:25 AMP.*

Lessons From My Dog

We often hear how bad habits can be very depleting in our lives. We also need to recognise that some habits, traditions and customs are good for us.

Bad habits can be very depleting in our lives. Some habits and traditions such as church participation, which was the custom of both Jesus and Paul, are actually very good for us.

Be like Jesus (Luke 4:16) and Paul (Acts 17:2) whose custom it was to go to church. Don't be like Doubting Thomas who was missing when Jesus turned up; nor like the 380 who missed the visitation of Holy Spirit in the Upper Room. Remember that in 1 Corinthians 15:6, Jesus appeared to more than five hundred at one time.

If the things of God such as prayer, reading God's Word, financial giving, personal and church worship and serving the Lord in church and in the world are not your custom, how can you expect to enter into the double portion?

All things are given to us by the Grace of God (that's His part); but we receive them by active faith (that's our part).

What I have said so far in regard to the double portion journey, is that it starts with salvation (Gilgal) and continues with discipleship in the local church (Bethel). The church and the relationships we build and learn from are fundamental to building strong faith in the Lord and His Word. This helps us mature as Christians and to learn how to walk by faith in all areas of life. (2 Corinthians 5:7).

(ii) Jericho, the place of overcoming adversity and opposition

The third place prophets Elijah and Elisha visited was Jericho, where Joshua and his army saw God flatten the city's walls as they obeyed His strategy for victory.

If we want the double portion, we've got to do things God's Way and we've got to walk by faith. For Joshua and his army, that included taking control of their own tongues. They marched around the city in silence. That way no negative talk about the battle was possible. In World War 2 there was a saying to warn people about the power of their tongues: "Loose lips sink ships."

Israel faced the enemy together, not alone, believing for the supernatural partnership of the Holy Spirit. When the battle was to be joined, they shouted confidently and fought like victors, not victims.

We've got to face our enemies, within and without, and believe God for the victory. As Christ's Church, we are to be the devil's nightmare, as we enforce the victory Jesus has won over the devil and all his works. Jesus is our Commander-in-Chief, which is how He revealed Himself to Joshua prior to the battle.

Let me also remind you of the principle found in James 4:7. You cannot defeat the enemy unless and until you are submitted to God.

(iii) Jordan, where miracles happen

The double portion journey starts with salvation, continues with discipleship in the local church, progresses by overcoming adversity and opposition and fourthly, it requires the believer to step into a lifestyle of faith that enables them to experience the favour of God and supernatural partnership of the Lord.

It is common for Spirit-filled preachers like myself to see the symbolism of Israel crossing the River Jordan into their Promised Land as representing receiving the baptism in the Holy Spirit, because crossing the Red Sea is interpreted as the type of becoming born again.

(a)   Through the example of Jesus, we learn the Jordan represents the place of experiencing an Open Heaven, the Father's Voice and the Power of Holy Spirit.

The River Jordan is where the ministry of Jesus started. Mark 1:9 tells us that Jesus was baptised both in water and in Holy Spirit and heard the affirming Voice of the Father at the River Jordan.

So, the River represents a place of an open Heaven. It speaks of Holy Spirit empowerment to do the work of the ministry that we have been called to do. The River Jordan is the launching place for every Christian to live a supernatural lifestyle. (Acts 1:8). It is the place where God opens our eyes and ears to the invisible world of Holy Spirit and the angels, as Jesus promised Nathaniel. (John 1:51).

Water baptism is symbolic of dying to the old worldly life and Holy Spirit baptism is representative of living in the new supernatural life of the Spirit. Sadly, many Christians today only know one baptism, not the two baptisms Jesus set as an example for us to follow. Jesus wants every Christian to be a supernatural son and servant of God. This is why He sent Holy Spirit on the day of Pentecost to give the church "power", Divine power. (Acts 1:8).

(b)   No turning back, at this final stage, from the Promised Land lifestyle of faith and supernatural Holy Spirit Partnership.

Both baptisms represent an attitude of no turning back, as did the crossing over of Joshua and the Jews.

The River Jordan also represents the final stage in the journey from the wilderness, the time of preparation, to the edge of the Promised Land and into the land of fulfilment.

According to 2 Kings 6:2 the River Jordan was the place where Elisha's faith and double portion anointing and spiritual authority was used to miraculously raise a borrowed axe head that had fallen into the murky river.

Just as the prophet threw in a stick, so you have to sow before you reap; you have to step out in faith; you have to do something in order to step into the supernatural and keep on doing it so that it becomes a lifestyle of Divine relationship and partnership between you and God.

Elisha inherited the double portion because he had the faith to pursue, to see and to do. It's interesting to note that when you compare the number of miracles associated with Elijah and Elisha in the Bible, you find that Elisha is credited with twice as many miracles as his mentor, Elijah. How often it is that the generation who stand on the shoulders of others achieves more than they did. The ceiling of the previous generation becomes the floor of their successors.

By contrast to Elisha, Esau didn't value God's promises, so he sold his double portion inheritance of the first-born son to his brother Jacob. He wanted food now. How many have missed out on their double portion, because they hunger for the immediate satisfaction of the things of this world?

Elisha also demonstrated holy boldness as he stepped out in faith after fulfilling the condition Elijah had specified would qualify him to receive the double portion.

He struck the water as he had seen Elijah do and boldly called out "where is the Lord God of Elijah?" In other words, he said to God: "I've done my bit, so Lord now it's Your turn; the ball is in Your court." In New Testament terms we would say: "Lord, I expect Divine action now, based on a covenant fulfilled by Jesus and on my obedience to the promises and principles of Your Word."

> *Where is the Lord God of Elijah? I've done my bit, so Lord now it's Your turn; the ball is in Your court. Lord, I expect Divine action now, based on a covenant fulfilled by Jesus and on my obedience to the promises and principles of Your Word.*

When you are not sure what to do to receive your miracle, do what you have been taught to do or what you have seen your mentors do. Every time, when you do what the Bible says, you can be sure God will do what the Bible says.

Elisha's first miracle of the parting of the River Jordan, teaches us this: there really are no "suddenlys" and certainly none that "just happen".

Jesus lived 30 years of preparation and learning the Word and being obedient. Then came the Voice and the Spirit. Most of the people in the upper room on the day of Pentecost had for three years given up everything to follow Jesus. Then, in obedience to Him, they spent 10 days and nights in the upper room, worshipping, praying, praising, waiting on the Lord, encouraging one another in the Scriptures. After that, the Spirit came in mighty power.

(iv) What is your lifestyle?

Are you in some kind of slavery or bondage situation within yourself or in life's circumstances? The Lord can set you free.

Are you wandering round and round in a spiritual wilderness, just staying alive, bored in your faith, doing nothing to fulfil God's covenant purposes and not receiving all His covenant blessings and resources?

Or are you a Promised Land Christian, who is not fazed by adversity or opposition? Are you getting on with what God has called you to do, whether you can see great fruit or not? If you are, take courage, because Galatians 6:9 tells you that if you do not grow weary in well doing, you will reap a harvest.

God has called you to be more than a conqueror. (Romans 8:37). That means you not only win for yourself but for others; and you do not conquer for yourself, but to set captives free so they can also be victorious, prosper and help others.

You double portion blessings, resources and miracles are on their way. Your victories are guaranteed by the victory of Jesus. You are a walking power-house for God, because Holy Spirit lives in you. You can make a difference in your world and in the lives of people around you, because as you step out in faith, Holy Spirit steps out with you.

What is one thing you have learned from this teaching?

What is one thing you can do to implement this teaching?

Faith Declaration:

I thank You Lord for enabling me to grow from faith to faith, strength to strength, glory to glory, victory to victory and anointing to anointing. By faith I step into my next level place in God. I believe for and speak into being the double portion plus of Heaven to be manifest in every area of my life, family and ministry in Jesus' Name. Lord I dedicate myself afresh to a life of true and full discipleship of following Jesus, according to Your Word and the leading of Your Spirit. I believe Your Senior and Supernatural Partnership will be in increasing evidence in my life, for the glory of my King, Jesus, in Whose Name I make this declaration. Amen.

34 Lessons from my Dog: a Wedding Message

How does our little dog manage to wrap two grown people around her little paw? Well, she does. Chloe, our Shih-Tzu, brings great joy into our lives and she also is a great teacher. Here are five life lessons that I learned from Chloe and shared at the wedding of our daughter Rebekah to her now-hubby Pete.

(i) The first thing dogs are known for is wagging their tails.

This tells us that we only have one life, so we need to make sure it includes having fun and showing appreciation.

In the words of the catchy hit song from the late eighties: "Don't worry, be happy."

Lessons From My Dog

Dogs demonstrate their joy so often and so obviously that they could never play professional poker, because whenever they got a good hand, everyone would know they were excited.

There's another thing more people should know about joy. The world thinks God is a killjoy, but the Gospel truth is that He is the Author and Source of joy.

The world thinks God is a killjoy, but the Gospel truth is that He is the Author and Source of joy.

These things I have spoken to you so that My joy may be in you, and that your joy may be made full.
John 15:11 NAS

Rejoice in the Lord always and again I say rejoice.
Philippians 4:4

When dogs wag their tails, they are often communicating something in addition to their joy. They are showing their love and affection for you.

Showing your love for your spouse and being affectionate is an important way to keep your romance alive.

Let your family, friends and colleagues know that you are happy to have them in your life. Affirm people who do a good job. Give thanks to whoever blesses you in some way.

(ii) The second thing dogs are known for is their loyalty and faithfulness.

I think that lesson speaks for itself. It reminds me of the traditional wedding vow "till death do us part."

Sadly, too many couples these days might as well say "until times get tough, or boring."

Faithfulness is so essential in every area of life. For example, in marriage and family, how many children's hearts have been broken because dad did not keep his promise? How many divorces, with all the heartache it causes for far more than two or three people, have been caused by unfaithfulness?

Another example is that, in the workplace, careers can be made or broken depending on a person's loyalty and trustworthiness.

Remember this: According to the parable of the talents, God expects and rewards faithfulness. He will also, when the time of final judgement comes, punish unfaithfulness. (Matthew 25:14–30).

(iii) "He who lies down with dogs, shall rise up with fleas."

My third doggy-lesson is based on the saying often attributed to Benjamin Franklin. It is about the negative impact wrong relationships can have on our lives.

> *Do not be misled: "Bad company corrupts good character."*
> *1 Corinthians 15:33*

The point is this: be very careful whom you allow to influence your life. In Jeremiah 15:19, the prophet was told to influence others and to not allow people to influence him. That was a mistake that the prophet Isaiah seems to have made, before his transformation and higher calling was birthed when he had a Divine encounter in the temple, in the year that King Uzziah died. (Isaiah 6:5).

Most of us have heard the saying: "*Hurt people hurt people.*" The fact is that negativity is catching. Thankfully, so are faith, confidence and joy.

If you want to have a happy marriage, don't bring any fleas home from work or anywhere else.

Lessons From My Dog

If you want to have a happy marriage, don't bring any fleas home from work or anywhere else.

Rather, be good for and to each other. Encourage one another to become bigger and better people.

(iv) "A dog who is chasing his lunch doesn't worry about his fleas."

The fourth lesson is this: Live passionately for the Divine purpose for which you were born. When you do, you won't sweat the small stuff that can be so annoying.

Life is about more than just an endless cycle of: sleep – work – eat – drink – play – sleep – work – eat – drink – play – sleep – work – eat – drink – play – sleep......

Make sure your life includes deeper and more significant things than just the routines of life on earth. Set yourselves some positive goals. Strive to excel and build a worthy legacy to share with and pass on to others. Pursue God's vision and purpose for your (short) life on Earth.

> *[10] And (find out NIV) try to learn [in your experience] what is pleasing to the Lord [let your lives be constant proofs of what is most acceptable to Him]. [15] Look carefully then how you walk! Live purposefully and worthily .., not as the unwise and witless, but as wise (sensible, intelligent people), [16] Making the very most of the time (you have) [buying up each opportunity ... NLT for doing good], because the days are evil. [17] Therefore do not be vague and foolish, nor act thoughtlessly, but understand and firmly grasp what the Lord wants you to do.*
>
> *Ephesians 5:10, 15–17 AMP.*

(v) Don't Make problems for Others; Accept Discipline; Reconcile Quickly

My last lessons can be seen by imagining what happens if and after Chloe disobeys these instructions:

- You shall not bury your bone in the dirt and then bring all that dirt into our nice clean home.

- You shall not chew on my new shoes just because the smell of the leather makes you think they are made of beef jerky.

- You shall not mistake our new green rug for grass and use it like male dogs do a lamp-post or a tree.

My three instructions to Chloe are a useful reminder that we should not create problems for other people to clean up, nor behave in a way that spoils someone else's day.

Here is another thought about what our behaviour should be when someone annoys us. As one doggie commentator wrote: by all means, let others know when they've invaded your territory; but avoid biting when a simple growl will do. In other words, don't over-react to people or things that annoy you.

> *17 Never pay back evil with more evil. Do things in such a way that everyone can see you are honourable. 18 Do all that you can to live in peace with everyone. 19 Dear friends, never take revenge. Leave that to the righteous anger of God. For the Scriptures say, "I will take revenge; I will pay them back," says the Lord..... 21 Do not be overcome by evil, but overcome evil with good.*
> Romans 12:17-19 NLT and 21 NIV

When dogs are disciplined, they are put outside. Almost immediately they turn around, wagging their tails because they want to come back in again. This teaches us to never allow offences and resentments to build up in our hearts. Be quick to reconcile when your relationships could be soured by something negative that has happened.

> *In your anger do not sin; do not let the sun go down while you are still angry.*
> *Ephesians 4:26*

The Book of Proverbs has much to say about the importance and benefits of accepting discipline. The Bible talks about the children of God being disciplined by our Heavenly Father, as well as children in family life being disciplined by their parents. There are other authorities who exercise discipline, such as the police and teachers and coaches.

Our attitude toward the discipline we receive determines whether it benefits us or not. Like adversity, it can either make us better or bitter people.

> "My son, do not make light of the Lord's discipline, and do not lose heart when he rebukes you, [6] because the Lord disciplines the one he loves, ... [11] *No discipline seems pleasant at the time, but painful. Later on, however, it produces a harvest of righteousness and peace for those who have been trained by it.*
> *Hebrews 11:5-6a, 11*

What is one thing you have learned from this teaching?

_____

What is one thing you can do to implement this teaching?

_____

Faith Declaration:

I thank You Lord for the love and joy I have in my life. I am so grateful for Your faithfulness to me and for helping me build quality relationships with others. I praise You for having a good and significant plan for me to enjoy and to fulfil. By Your grace and my faith I choose to forgive and forget the things that threaten to ruin my relationships and steal my joy. By faith I step into Your good, acceptable and perfect plan for my life, in Jesus' Name. Amen. Help me Lord to accept discipline and counsel in a positive and mature and humble way, so I might benefit from it, as You desire. Anoint me to not cause problems for other people. I declare that I am a good disciple of Jesus and, by the grace given to me and in the power of Holy Spirit, I am a problem-solver, not a problem-maker, to the glory of God.

_____

ABOUT THE AUTHOR

Nick Watson has been happily married to Lynne since 1970. They have 3 children, Kylie, Simon and Rebekah; 4 grandchildren Katie, Rennick, Craig and Aiden; and 1 great-granddaughter, Riley.

Nick is the Founder, Principal Prophet, Author and Teacher, and People Builder of Prophetic Power Ministries.

He was for years the Senior Pastor of Bayside Christian Family (Apostolic) Church, a thriving Spirit-filled church in Brisbane, Queensland. Australia.

Nick has been a recognised prophet in the Apostolic Church Australia for more than 25 years. He has served in various denominational leadership roles.

Nick has preached and prophesied throughout Australia and overseas, with a signs-following ministry.

YOUR FEEDBACK

If this book "Lessons from My Dog: Faith-Lifters that Bless and Build Believers" has encouraged your faith, please share your testimony with us at the email address below.

Contact Nick Watson

If you desire to contact Nick concerning a ministry engagement at your church, group, camp or leaders' event please visit our website:

www.youcanprophesy.com

 www.facebook.com/nickjwatson.ycp

email: youcanprophesy@gmail.com

OTHER BOOKS by Nick Watson

Faith Food Snack Pack – Overcoming

Faith Food Snack Pack – Good News

Faith Food Snack Pack – Healthy Soul

Faith Food Snack Pack – Holy Spirit

You Can Prophesy – Supernatural. Simple. Safe.

Endorsements for Nick's first book "You Can Prophesy – Supernatural. Simple. Safe."

USA

Thanks for writing this Book, Pastor Nick. It is a "Tour de force", a workshop for those desiring more of the visibility of God in their daily lives!

Rev. Dr. Michael R. Bingham,

Deer Park, Texas U.S.A.

Nick Watson gives practical steps and understanding in how to live a naturally supernatural prophetic lifestyle that will transform the world around you. I would encourage you to read this book, and then do it!

Kevin Dedmon,

Evangelist, Bethel Church, Redding, California.
Author of "The Ultimate Treasure Hunt: Supernatural Evangelism Through Supernatural Encounters".

Nick Watson is to be thanked for contributing a very encouraging and insightful tome regarding the whole art of intimacy with the person of God. Chapters 7 and 11 in and of themselves, are worth the price of the book in helping us to understand the variety of ways God speaks and, then, how to rightfully divide the true and the false, the sacred and the profane. It is a privilege for me to endorse this book.

Marc Dupont

Mantle of Praise Ministries
Author of "Becoming the Friend of God" and Lead Author of "New Testament Prophetic Ministry – Biblical Principles concerning Ethics and Protocols Ethics".

Nick, well done! I was fully impressed by how thorough and practical your book is. Your understanding and explanation of the prophetic ministry would help anyone getting started in prophetic ministry and would be a great check-up for someone who is experienced in this ministry. May God bless this teaching!

Wally Odum

pastored one of Virginia Beach's first mega-churches.
He has an international apostolic ministry to pastors and church leaders.

Nick's easy to read style and frank up to date way of speaking make clear what he is saying. It is easy to see the prompting of the Holy Spirit through Nick to release the prophetic in a greater way. May God use this book to stir up that gifting he gave to the church.

Paul Palmer

Heart For The Harvest, USA. Prophet and Church Planter

Australian Ministry Leaders

I enjoyed reading Nick's great book. It is an excellent resource for those who desire to understand the Gift of a Prophet and the definition of Prophecy. I have known Nick as a friend and Prophet for over 25 years. His vast experience, and wisdom gained over these years in ministry is clearly reflected in depth of this book.

As you read this book, you will experience Nick's passion, wealth of insight and revelation into the realm of the Prophetic. I highly recommend you read this book and absorb the wealth of insight and wisdom, supported by the truth expounded from scripture. The Kingdom will greatly benefit from His book.

Graham Harris

Senior minister I A M house of worship
Founder of International Apostolic Ministries World Wide

I would recommend that all church leaders have this book as a reference on the prophetic. It is a refreshing, mature, Biblical overview of the deep well of prophetic ministry. This book is greatly beneficial to the novice as well as the seasoned prophet. I highly recommend this book to the global church as a safe, simple book on the supernatural ministry of the prophetic. Thank you Nick for your insight and effort. Well done.

Royree Jensen

Senior Pastor, River of Life church, Logan City
Director and Apostolic Leader, Harvest International Ministries Australia.

Nick demystifies prophetic ministry and presents difficult concepts in brilliant simplicity. I recommend this book as a gem for anyone wanting to develop in the prophetic gift or to simply understand it more.

Paul Pardede,

Lead Pastor,
Westlife Church, Assemblies of God, Springfield. Qld.

This is a very timely book for the Body of Christ! I have known Pastor Nick Watson for a number of years, and after seeing him minister at my church, I have always had the utmost respect for him as a great Aussie Leader. He has also raised up many and trained them to use their spiritual gifts for the Lord. Nick unpacks the topics in this book in an easy to read manner.

Matt Prater,

Senior Pastor New Hope Brisbane Church and host of Historymakers Radio & TV. Chairman of the Australian National Day of Prayer and Fasting.

It is my pleasure to endorse your book. This is a much needed tool for both churches and leaders in stewarding the prophetic gift. Written with candour and wisdom, Nick's book is a delightful read that will encourage you and give you tools to apply and activate prophecy in your own life. This book is a gift to the body of Christ written by one whose prophetic integrity is well known. Thank-you Nick. Australia has been waiting for a book like this.

Katherine Ruonala

Author, "Living in the Miraculous: How God's Love is Expressed through the Supernatural"
Senior Leader, Glory City Churches International

I have known Nick for a number of years and hold him in high regard concerning the prophetic ministry. I believe Nick has written a winner here, he has hit a 'Home Run'. This is something that can straighten out wrong concepts and misunderstandings. I love practical, down-to-earth teaching.

In a nutshell I am most happy to recommend Nick's book, I think it is a very practical and much needed tool to help a lot of people and clear up a lot of the mess!

Apostle Dr. Col Stringer

Author of 20 Christian books, including "On Eagles Wings" and "800 Horsemen." President, International Convention of Faith Ministers

Apostolic Church Australasia

This is an insightful, well researched and easy to read book – well done, Nick. I commend this contribution to our understanding of the ways of God to every genuine seeker of truth.

Timothy W Jack

Director of Ministries Apostolic Church Australia

Nick Watson insightfully, inspirationally, practically and most of all with revelatory clarity, shows us how to prophesy and interact with prophecy and with those who prophesy. Thank you, this is a great tool for the Body of Christ.

Apostle Nick Klinkenberg

Network Leader, Church Planter, Author,
Vision Churches International.
Acts Churches NZ

After some years of working alongside Prophet Nick Watson, it is very clear that he is fully committed to the gift God has given him. Like Elijah, he has experienced the highs and lows. This has produced a Word based expose of the Prophet and prophetic ministry that is Biblical, balanced and refreshingly easy to digest. Even though this book will relate exceptionally well to today's generation, I believe it will stand the test of time assisting generations that follow to understand, operate and value this gift.

Apostle Brad Otto,

Network Leader, member of Australian Apostolic National Leadership Team, Snr. Minister, Southland Christian Centre, Gold Coast

I've read the book and have to say, I was impressed!

The early chapters are clear and to the point, confirming the truth of your teaching, which I have had the privilege of hearing for over thirty years. They cover comprehensively what I have learned during those years. The later chapters took me deeper into the world of the prophet, and I can appreciate a lot better now what that role entails. Awesome stuff.

All in all I think this book will become a major resource for other pastors teaching on the topic of prophecy. Well done, Nick. I feel proud to have had a preview.

Elizabeth Scrimshaw

Bayside Christian Family Church member

All I can say is that it is brilliant. A prophetic resource that is so needed. Easy to read, love the stories, the honesty and so much amazing truth. Honestly Nick it is great, really great. I think it is a winner. Be encouraged. Such practical insight.

Lynette Tobin,

Lynette Tobin Ministries,

National and international Apostolic/Prophetic ministry.

Printed by Libri Plureos GmbH in Hamburg, Germany